Reflections, Memories, Thoughts and Observations

Collected Works

Paul M. Ryan

The contents of this work, including, but not limited to, the accuracy of events, people, and places depicted; opinions expressed; permission to use previously published materials included; and any advice given or actions advocated are solely the responsibility of the author, who assumes all liability for said work and indemnifies the publisher against any claims stemming from publication of the work. Any references to real persons, whether living or dead, or to events or places in the short stories are purely coincidental and a product of the author's imagination.

All Rights Reserved
Copyright © 2020 by Paul M. Ryan

No part of this book may be reproduced or transmitted, downloaded, distributed, reverse engineered, or stored in or introduced into any information storage and retrieval system, in any form or by any means, including photocopying and recording, whether electronic or mechanical, now known or hereinafter invented without permission in writing from the publisher.

Dorrance Publishing Co
585 Alpha Drive
Suite 103
Pittsburgh, PA 15238
Visit our website at *www.dorrancebookstore.com*

ISBN: 978-1-6470-2012-5
eISBN: 978-1-6470-2031-6

Contents

PART I - - POEMS 1

War 3
    Winds of War 4
    Easter in Vietnam 5
    A Light at the End of the Tunnel 6
    A Reflection 7
    Wartime Remembrance 8
    The Soldier Within 9
    Ten-Hut! 10
    Love Choices 11
    Respite 12
    Taking Leave 13
    A Lover's Question 14

Love 15
    A Gift of Love 17
    The Magic of Love 18
    Fantasy 19
    A Christmas Wish 20
    Love Loss 21
    A Season's Passing 22

Philosophy and Politics 23
    Enigma 25
    To My Inspiration 26
    small world 27
    Masters of the Earth 28
    People vs. Businessman-Politician 29
    Ideology vs. Reality 30
    Poisonous Pedagogy 31
    Tabula Rasa 32
    Risk and Freedom 33
    'Twas the Night of Comeuppance 35

Wasteland 37
    I   Trees 37
    II Animals 38
    III Earth, Air, and Water 39
    IV Man 40
The Road 41
Snowflake 43
Leadership 44
One Idea of a Friend 45
Nancy's Wall 46
State of Disunion 47
The I Factor 48
Division of America 49
The Squad 51
Omar 53

College 55
Meditations of a Bored Anthropology Student 57
Beach Bum Bradley 58
Mystery Girl #1 59
Mystery Girl #2 60
Philosophy 61
Twenty-two 62
Admonishment 63
Study Break 64
Comeuppance 65

Family 67
Carrie A-Writing 69
Robert the Comic 70
Ode to Jay's Retirement 71

PART II - - SHORT STORIES 73

The Poem: An American Tragedy 75
A Sunday Visitation 78
Word Smiting 80
Calizuela 82
Magical Dirt 84
Reflections of a Psychological Garden of Eden 85
Shoot Up 90
Opportunity Lost 92
Red Flag 95

PART III - - ESSAYS 97

Abortion Paradigms 99
Abuse 101
Angel of God 103
    Introduction 103
    Woman on the Prescott Bus 103
    Darting Across 14th Avenue 104
    Runaway Car 105
    Essay on St. Brendan the Navigator 105
    Another Stranger 106
    Eel River Crossing 106
    Rocket Explosion at Long Binh, Vietnam 106
    Life Mission 107
    Pieces of My Life Puzzle 107
    Location of Father 108
    Salvage from Rogue River 108
    The Bear 108
    Medical Interventions 110
    Diaphragmatic Hernia 110
    Lymphoma 110
    Bar Exam 111
    Family 112

Book Selections 113
Choosing Freedom 114
Coping with Adversity 116
Letting Go and Adapting to Change 118
Tolstoy: A Rebuttal 122
Adhering to the Enemy 124
Ant Confederacy 126
Ejection of God from the Public Square 128
Times of Our Life 129
Disrespectful Celebrity Activity 131
The Fart Heard 'Round the World 132
The Bastardization of Language .133
The Hare and the Hounds 138

PART IV - - SONG, PARODIES, AND HUMOR 139

America (My Country 'Tis of Me) .141
Taliban Parody 144
Unions: The Sound of Fright 145
Christmas in Smoke 146
Cat and Mouse 148
Who's the Dummy? 149

PART V - - DEDICATION 151

Advice for a Happy Life 153
Glory 154

PART I
POEMS

WAR

Winds of War

The wind is blowing hard today
Making leaves and branches sway.
I wonder if a message lies
Within this turmoil from the skies.

Things are happening on our sphere
'Twould keep a god from coming near.
The things about which I am speaking
Range from war to a faucet leaking.

Bullets have ravaged flesh for some time
And this I think is a terrible crime
For war that's fought without a cause
Violates the best of laws.

China threatens the world with numbers.
(Russia calls it a giant who slumbers.)
Nations idle, anticipating
The day when they'll start escalating.

World leaders play a guessing game
And send their soldiers to kill and maim
Thousands of men who want no fight
But only a free untroubled night.

One day it will be too late:
We'll not be able to stop our fate
'Cause the world itself will be corroded
By fallout from a bomb exploded.

Political winds are blowing frightfully,
Shaking the world and its people mightily.
I'd rather have a gentle breeze
Comforting men on thankful knees.

November 1968

Easter in Vietnam

Here in a land of war—
A day called Easter in other lands
I lay on my cot.
My thoughts of Easter and home—
Are dominated with thoughts of you:

Your tender, glowing smile
Is with me all the while.
Your young laughing eyes
Ensure my sunny skies.

The thought of your lips
And of chocolate chips
Remind me of you
And the things that you do.

Here from afar
I recall how you are.
For the moments we've had
I'll forever be glad.

You're warm and loving as woman can be.
You really mean a lot to me.
So with these words I hope you know
Our love can only upwards grow

In the moments we've shared
You've known that I cared.
My love is strong—
Will remain so for long.

The day, a symbol of joy and love,
I raise my eyes to the god above
Whom I thank for these reflections
Unmarred by any imperfections

April 1969

A Light at the End of the Tunnel

I didn't want to leave you—
But there's a war going on.
Like most men I had
plans and dreams;
I've had my share of trouble
too.

But what is a man without trouble?
Battles often make men
of boys.
And how can one learn if not by trial?

Who can mold his character
without mistakes—or
love, or even fight without
losing something of himself?
But by losing does he not
gain something in return
Awareness?

Now my thoughts return to
days of past happiness—
To thoughts of love, happy times, friends
and you

And someday, when this war is over—
I'll return to my plans
—my mistakes
—my hopes
—my trials
—my dreams…
and you.

October 1969

A Reflection

For every man there comes
a time of silence:
a quiet hour of a
wakeful night—
when thoughts of the past
bring an honest awareness.

Such a time is found
sometimes in the midst of turmoil—
like the serenity at the
center of a hustling hurricane.
Or in a war.

There is a war going on
around me.
Yet I am calm, and in
my serenity—my security
the meaning of past actions
and mistakes assume
a certain clarity—honesty.

There is no need to
assume here or to
let petty grievances
influence
Thoughts, feelings, judgments, loves.

June 1969

Wartime Remembrance

Men lay on their battle-packs
Rereading letters that meant so much…
Talking of past times … quietly,
So that "Charlie" will not hear…
Or … gazing at the fading light.

The muffled snores…
of tired men
Filter through the brush.
The sound of Zorba's laughter
Would be welcome now.

Some write letters
Wanting to talk—wondering…
What hands are invading his dreams
Knowing that he is gone now
From her mind…
Maybe to return again on Monday,
Or maybe Tuesday.

Once again, the mind turns
To tomorrow's battle.

March 1969

The Soldier Within

Smile!

I'll tell you of the good times
I've had in the Army.
Don't ask about the bad times.
I've never felt a smile fade
so quickly—
with the memories of mud, gunfire
and the steel pot.
These are things only the soldier
can understand, remember.
He finds...manhood...
A certain satisfaction in conquering
—The impossible
—The cut hands
The wounded pride.

A man in the field knows...
What he is...
Who he is...
A man or a boy.

Things a woman can only know
in her heart—
without asking.

November 17, 1968

Ten-Hut!

ATTENTION!
The captain is coming.
"Your boots are not shined."
But that doesn't matter;
The trails are mined.

Inspecting your weapon—
"There's rust on the bore!"
"Stabbed a man yesterday.
Sure he was sore."

The captain has stopped
To look at your brass.
Hasn't been polished—
Makes him act crass.

What does it matter
How good we all look?
Fighting is dirty;
But we live by the book.

October 1969

Love Choices

A Chance…
For What…
To Love…
The most difficult chance…Choice?
Maybe.

A Touch…warm
A song we both like
Two shadows…
A ski-lodge fire…
An infant's cry at night…and
Reaching out in bed.

To love…
Choice?

Oneness…hurt
The song we liked
Heard far away now…
In the back of the mind somewhere.

One shadow…one lamp
And one novel.

No shadow…no light
And one M16
Songs fade quickly sometimes.

November 1969

Respite

I stopped atop a mountain once
To gaze at the world below,
All was calm and peaceful there.
I had no wish to go.

The snow was fresh and terribly bright.
The sun and breeze were both just right.
My spirits were lifted because of the view
And I wished that you could share it, too.

The lake below so deep and blue
And the cloud-capped hills beyond—
Stirred my soul so fresh and new
To yearn for the calm of a peaceful pond.

Wars rage the world around
Here—the silent, peaceful sound,
Would that the world could see this place
And erase the wars that scar its face.

January 1970

Taking Leave

Times of love pass quickly
before leaving.
Tears won't help
It always goes that way.
Many men have come—
Gone.
And many have come back again

So let us laugh together—
Make the night one
with the day.

Save the tears…
the prayers
for the endless nights
that follow.

And curse the need for war
that separates the night
from the day.

December 1969

A Lover's Question

What was the meaning of that first note, that first smile?
Was there any meaning in that makeshift tent,
sleeping under the meager protection of a nylon sail?
Who can say what the meaning of wine is for another person,
or a poem that meant so much to the poet and not a damn thing to his lover?

What was the meaning of life and love for Jezebel and Cleopatra?
Did life hold any meaning for them or did their passions rule the minds and
hearts of a nation?

What comes first in the minds of some women—
Do they love or do they pretend to love or are they ever sure of what love is;
Or, has it a different meaning for them?
I don't know what it means when women care or when they don't care.

1968

LOVE

A Gift of Love

I wandered alone by the evening sea.
There was peace and solitude
Peace in the beauty of the darkening clouds
against an orange sky.
Yet there was no one beside me and I felt the emptiness.

I walked along the boardwalk
Where there were many people—
So many people
But still no peace or companionship.

Then I found love…
Someone who give me peace
pleasure
understanding
love.
But instead I found pain.

So I returned to the solitude of the sea and myself
and wondered why.
When next I sought love
I gave counsel
pleasure
joy
myself.
So we went to the sea and shared its beauty and its peacefulness.

October 1965

The Magic of Love

There is frost on our window
this morning.
No heat in our tiny cabin
—but the warmth of a
newfound love protects us from
the cold outside—
And our arguments push
the coldness from our hearts—and
open them up for still
More love and pain.

I love the cold, wet snow
on a winter day.
I love the warm even more
because of the cold.

Love expels the cold of an unloved heart;
And the cold makes room
—for the warm.
The new warmth makes the
cold more endurable.

Help me to adapt to the warmth
of your love;
And in winter when I rush
in from the cold—
Give me your hand—
I may never want the cold again.

1968

Fantasy

What a perfect delight I took at the sight!
Her face so fair, her hips so trim.
Her head, her hair were all just right!
Oh, if only a maiden and I her knight!

Behold the woman! Behold the man!
Fly to each other as fast as we can.
And ne'er will we part for ne'er we can.
For she is my woman and I am her man.

1966

A Christmas Wish

Christmas is coming, or so they say.
Time to make merry in the usual way.
We'll go to the mountain in my cabin to stay.
We'll light up the fire and watch our kids play.
That's what I'm hoping for, now, today.

But this is a dream that is far away.
I have no cabin wherein to stay.
I have no children who run and play.
And my wife I have yet to meet someday.
But still I can hope it will happen this way.

1965

Love Loss

A black, threatening cloud
opened its belly
and washed away
the imprint of our body
in the sand.
And the prints there were no more.
Still the two bodies exist
separated
yet still entwined.

A dark cloud
threatening and black
passed over our soul
and washed away the
beauty
that once shone there.
The two who laughed together laugh no more.

October 19, 1968

A Season's Passing

Where have the warm winds wandered?
Cold, crisp crosswinds lash about.
The soft white suds of summer—
Now omens of rain and overflowing spouts.

The happy memories of summer last:
Now a source of agony and pain.
The warm wonder of her soft skin
is but a fading image through the misty rain.

May 1969

PHILOSOPHY AND POLITICS

Enigma

Some say I have an angel on my shoulder;
others say that my luck is the worst.
The truth of the matter is that I am a
truly complicated man
and that I appear as many things to many people.
Still, I am very simple for all my complexity
and easy to understand.

I am not different from other men
and yet I can't help but be different
for I am a unique person
who reacts to each other human
as each presents himself to me.

Perhaps I have an angel, perhaps a devil.
No one really knows because no one perceives
me as does anyone else.
And therefore, they cannot agree
unless I appear to all of them as I appear to me.

1967

To My Inspiration

When I am all alone at home
and feeling sad and lost and blue;
I take my pen and write a poem.
It seems the only thing to do.

It's times like this that I think best.
It's times like this I worry, too.
It's times like this that I am blessed
With inspirations from God through you.

1966

small world

The world is growing smaller
I can talk across the sea.
But I hardly know my neighbor
He's a stranger to me.

There is love in the world
But it's hard for you to find.
You cannot feel what's in your heart
For you have blown your mind.

A man has fallen in the street
I pretend I do not see.
Guess he's had too much to drink;
I'll not be neighborly.

1971

Masters of the Earth

The leaves are falling on the ground.
They're doing it without a sound.
The trees on which they did abound.
Endure their loss without a sound.

There's a lesson here that's very plain.
All of nature is an endless chain
Of life and death and birth again.
All but one creature does not complain,
And it has a heart, a soul, and a brain.

1963

People vs. Businessman-Politician

There is hope in the world
That all men will be free.
        "Oh, may they all be equal
        If they all look just like me."

Oh, the color doesn't matter
But the attitude toward life.
        "Why not go to Africa
        And get yourself a wife."

There is hate in the world.
It's not hard for you to find.
You cannot feel what's in your heart
For you have closed your mind.

        "Oh, why must we have peace abroad?
        My business will be killed.
        If I cannot make the weapons
        The people can't be billed."

June 1967

Ideology vs. Reality

The boy was trained to be a man:
A man who would not kill or maim.
But he was called to fight a war
To avenge his country's name.

The woman was trained to be a mother:
A healer of hurts; soother of emotions.
But her child was called away from home
And the mother left to confront her notions.

The man was trained to be a healer,
To conquer ills and pain.
But he was called to remove a growth
To save a woman's life again.

The woman was trained to be respectful of life
To bear her children and be a good wife.
Confronted with illness and family strife
She had a fetus removed with a knife.

The world is neither black nor white.
The world is neither dark nor light.
Choices are neither wrong nor right.
Choices are neither dark nor bright.

Poisonous Pedagogy

A child was born some years ago
With great potential and room to grow.
His body grew tall, and big and strong
But his soul went unnurtured by kind word or song.

In all his endeavors he behaved as a child—
His spirit self-serving, his temper most wild.
He heard neither reason, nor wisdom of years.
His needs unmet, he tossed tantrums and jeers.

His emotions repressed, he could not comprehend
How expressions of feeling help spirits to mend.
He could not respond to expressions of feeling
Without being threatened and frightened, unfeeling.

In relentless pursuit of complete domination
He did deeds men thought were an abomination.
For in seeking such power against any odds
He silently slipped to a role of the gods.

His child was born some years ago
With great potential and room to grow.
That child grew tall, and big, and strong
But he was taught neither right nor wrong.

Decisions are guesses toward best resolution
Where no clear rules offer easy solution.
Where no kind souls offer any ablution.
To make a decision is to live revolution.

When ideology collides with reality,
one must formulate a compromised solution
which will have far-reaching consequences
no matter what the decision.

March 26, 1990

Tabula Rasa

The child is born an empty vessel
A sacred trust of those who shape him.
His head is filled from earliest days
With thoughts and teachings of cultural ways.

His mind is shaped for various aims
By those who o'rtake it, staking their claims.
In boyhood he learns to give grownups their due
To be trustworthy, loyal and obedient, too.

These patterns developed so early and fast
May not always be so honorable and right
And to change it around the poor child must fight.
If only the teaching could be honest and true
And the teachers learn more of the good they could do.

February 14, 1990

Risk and Freedom

To think and to dare to arrive at conclusions is to risk being labelled unorthodox or heretical.

To expose ideas or dreams before others is to risk their loss; to risk criticism and rejection.

To expose one's innermost feelings to another is to risk being misunderstood.

To joke is to risk appearing frivolous.

To dress up and to be well-groomed is to risk appearing haughty, arrogant or vain.

To invest in friendships is to risk gossip.

To laugh is to risk appearing the fool.

To cry is to risk appearing weak or sentimental.

To reach out for another is to risk involvement.

To love is to risk not being loved in return.

To climb is to risk falling.

To live is to risk dying.

To make a change is to risk losing the comfort of established living patterns.

To believe is to risk disenchantment.

To hope is to risk disillusionment.

To strive for a goal is to risk failure.

But risks must be taken, because the greatest threat to life is to risk nothing.

Those who risk nothing have nothing worth losing.

Those who risk nothing do not live life, but merely
watch life flow past them.
They may avoid suffering and sorrow, but they
cannot learn, feel, change, grow, love, live.

Chained by their attitudes or frozen by indecision or fear,
they are slaves to inaction; they have forfeited their freedom to participate
in life to the fullest measure.

Only a person who risks is free.

Only a person who risks is alive.

April 7, 1990

'Twas the Night of Comeuppance

'Twas a night of comeuppance, when all through the cave
Al Qaeda was cursing the Land of the Brave;
Machine guns were aimed the entrance with care,
In hopes that our soldiers soon would be there.

Al Qaeda were nestled all smug in belief,
That our solders would soon come to terrible grief;
Osama in his turban, Omar in his gown,
Had finished their scheming and had just settled down.

When outside the cave there arose such thunder,
They sprang to their feet tearing garments asunder.
Away from the entrance they flew in a flash,
As a bomb exploded, spewing up rocks and ash.

Shadows on cave walls portended the future
Showed pictures of bleeding and bashing and sutures,
When, what to their wondering eyes should appear,
But a swarming of solders in full fighting gear.

With so fearsome a leader, the man was no wuss,
They knew in a moment it must be George Bush.
More rapid than eagles the troopers they came,
they fired, and shouted, and called them by name.

"Now, OSAMA! Now, OMAR! and mostly Bin Laden
Now is the hour; there'll be no more hidin'.
To the back of the cave! down the long narrow hall!
We'll dash away! dash away! dash away you all!"

And then, in a twinkling, they heard the sound
Of the whining and spinning of each spent round.
As they dropped to the floor, and were turning around,
Down the shaft saw Osama turn with a bound.

He was dressed all in robes, from his head to his foot,
And his clothes were all tarnished with ashes and soot;

A bundle of weapons were strung on his back,
And he looked like a burglar with a full booty sack.

His eyes—how they smirked! His forehead was furrowed!
His cheeks they were burnished, his nose much narrowed!
His droll little mouth was drawn down like a bow,
And his beard was all dirty like soot-covered snow.

A renegade rifle he held tight in his grip,
And over his shoulder a full ammo clip;
He looked coldly evil, yet seemed very calm,
He'd clearly kill anyone with nary a qualm.

He was churly and sour, a right nasty fellow,
It could never be said that Osama was mellow;
With his hand on the bolt; with a twist of his head,
Soon gave us to know that he wanted us dead

He spoke not a word, but went straight to his work,
Aimed right at us; and recoiled with a jerk,
As his finger pulled back, with his weapon full loaded,
But surprise of surprises, the chamber exploded.

His soul, oh so tarnished, flew to straight into hell;
Looked about for his virgins; thinking life would be swell.
The last thing we heard was Beelzebub saying,
"No virgins for you: There's no use in your praying."

December 2001

WASTELAND

I
Trees

A seedling sprouted and began to grow
Some two thousand years or so ago.
Soon there were forests of redwood giants
Seeking nothing more than nature's compliance.

For hundreds of years the trees were respected.
No one sawed, chopped or had them dissected.
The world was simpler, despite evolution
But then came industry's revolution.

We came needful of paper: "More, if you please!"
And 'gan lusting after those big redwood trees.
We cut them and chopped them till none were left standing
But we had our needs so we kept on demanding.

Hearty log cutters asked: "What can we do—
Now that we have no more forests to screw?"
Lumberjacks idle, no work for their saws
Just had to abandon their unholy cause.

Hearty log cutters could not reason why
Nature had left their business to die.
They cursed the fact that trees grow so slow,
That their industry's captains had no place to go.

But none of us has cause for complaint.
We use paper products with little restraint.
We hunger for paper in various forms
And use it unwisely without any norms.

We plunder and pillage each precious resource.
It seems we have not a shred of remorse.
The trees, a valued asset of Nature, of course
Against odds of Man have no recourse.

II
Animals

The dolphin is slaughtered in ways most unfair.
If it happened to us our tempers would flare.
It seems no species is free from extinction.
For some the killing is source of distinction.

Behemoths are hunted for ivory sabers.
Whales are gutted for oil and tapers.
Animals blessed with beautiful fur
Are slaughtered *en masse* as a "gift for her"!

The mighty bison which once roamed the plain
Is no longer found, as most have been slain.
The baldheaded eagles which once their wings spread
Do so no longer because they're all dead.

The condor once flew so stately and black
His species likewise not free from attack.
The grizzlies that drank from a mountain lakeshore
Have been tracked by hunters and killed by the score.

The Florida black wolf who once roamed in that state
Cannot be found in his natural state.
The Bengal tiger with its stately strips
No longer makes his scavenging trips.

Profit margins demand our resources.
No creatures are safe, be they foxes or horses.
The spotted owl with its hoot and its holler
Could not care less if he brings top dollar.

But none of us has cause for complaint.
We use animal products with little restraint.
We hunger for meat and skins all the more
And only complain when they're not in the store.

We plunder and pillage each precious resource.
It seems we have not a shred of remorse.

Animals, valued assets of Nature, of course
Against odds of Man have no recourse.

III
Earth, Air, and Water

The ozone layer is thinning and balding
Allowing sunrays to pass, hot and scalding.
All of this due to Man's use of machine
Driven by pistons and crude gasoline.

Industrial stacks how they billow and spew
Oxides and chlorides to name just a few.
Acid rain effaces mountains and flowers
And stopping this threat is beyond Man's powers.

Exhaust of machines pollutes our air.
Poison is sprayed with nary a care.
Sewage is spilled in our rivers and oceans
But we just lay by applying our lotions.

Farm crops are dusted and sprayed for pests
And this is done with a great deal of zest.
The residue gushes from fields to rivers
And those who drink it get sick to their livers.

Fishes and cattle get sick from such stew
And we who eat them become ill, too.
The food chain is weakened with each new concoction.
Just to begin a solution, we'd expire from exhaustion.

But none of us has cause for complaint.
We abuse our earth with little restraint.
We need our world and all that it offers
And what do we care if we fill rich men's coffers.

We plunder and pillage each precious resource.
It seems we have not a shred of remorse.
The earth, a valued asset of Nature, of course
Against odds of Man has no recourse.

IV
Man

To Man was given the run of this sphere
To use its gifts wisely, its stores to revere.
As usage increases with mass escalation
Resources diminish in every nation.

Man himself should be first to preserve
Those things he needs as well as deserves.
They will not last if he does not conserve
With utmost sincerity, commitment and nerve.

For it will take effort and oh so much courage
To end the slaughter, and hunters discourage;
Lest someday this glorious planet will die—
A barren wasteland forever to lie.

What once will have been a world of plenty
Will have been sold for a ten or a twenty.
And all of the riches so richly bestowed
Will have been traded for dead vaults of gold.

The last resource is Man and his reason
But even with Man there's a killing season.
We kill ourselves with weapons and drugs.
With ourselves as with Nature we're hopeless thugs.

But none of us has cause for complaint.
We abuse each other with little restraint.
We ravish our planet and all that is in it.
We don't make the effort to preserve and defend it.

We plunder and pillage each precious resource.
It seems we have not a shred of remorse.
And Man, a valued asset of Nature, of course
Against odds of men has no recourse.

August 5, 1990

The Road

The road was long and narrow.
One of three ways I could choose.
Advised to choose the middle road—
Was told I could not lose.

The middle way was nicely paved—
Painted signs to show the way.
Its well-worn grooves foretold
How each should replicate the mold.

The middle path, the comfort zone:
Proceed with automatic eye—
Foreclose any deviation from the norm
And live unblinkingly until I die.

The right way lay beyond the paved;
A path of dirt and stone and weed.
Not maintained for travelers
Thought not to have the need.

The right-path traveler was on his own
To negotiate the way
Through bushes, leaves and flowers and creeks
And to tarry as he may.

There were no signs to fetter him
He had to think things through.
The only guides were in his head—
Conservative point of view.

The left-path traveler likewise left
To negotiate the way
Through bushes, leaves and flowers and creeks
And to tarry as he may.

There were no signs to fetter him.
He had to think things through.
The only guides were in his head—
The liberal point of view.

The right or the left, which 'ere I chose
I'd be free to strike my beat.
To the right or left, which 'ere I chose
Determined by my own feet.

I tried each road in turn, you see
And found the middle not for me.
The right and the left appealed the more.
Each step was life lived so much more.

September 9, 1990

Snowflake

Snowflake was formed in a cloud in the sky—
One of a kind, her beauty most high.
She drifted down for perhaps a mile
Enjoying the view and wearing a smile.

She met with the wind who blew her around
Sometimes blew up and sometimes down
He twirled her and hurled her, a spin and a twirl.
They danced together like a boy and a girl.

She plummeted downward through damp air and sky
Further and further from her start up so high;
Wafted through clouds: some were dark, some were bright,
Through darkness of rain and into sunlight.

Her journey near finished she wafted on down
Toward a blanket of snow that lay on the ground.
She settled down, her journey now done
To take time to herself to enjoy the sun.

The coldness thwarted her bid for some fun
And kept her from feeling the warmth of the sun.
When the sun shined through, he melted her down
And into a teardrop that sank in the ground.

September 8, 1990

Leadership

Leadership was defined to us
The reason should be clear:
Our mission is to free the world
From sinfulness and fear.

A leader is a friend to all.
This fact should not be strange.
For being one in Christ, you see
Includes the world in range.

True friendship is the secret which
Enables one to lead.
It caters to each person
Who finds himself in need.

In the face of trial and hardship
True friendship will not falter
When we are helped by Him
Whom we find upon the altar.

"Other awareness" you'll find is the key
To effective leadership certainly.
Leadership can be effected
Even if you're not elected.

A leader extends himself to his neighbors.
With an open mind and an open heart.
Each of us can be like this
If each of us will do his part.

Courage and discipline are integral part
Of this most important of the arts.
And if we do as we've been told
All of us shall become more bold.

1961

One Idea of a Friend

A friend is a magical fellow
Who listens to you when you bellow.
But much more than that
With him you can spat—
Unburden what's under your hat.

He'll speak to you freely
'Cause he loves you really.
He won't spare your feeling—
May send your head reeling
He'll do all the dealing.

And all of its just.
He does what he must:
Sees you in trouble
Perhaps seeing double
Help break you out of your bubble.

You may hate him forever
And your friendship you sever.
But since he is wise
He won't compromise
Or reduce you to your proper size.

He'll expect no return,
Though for it he'll yearn.
And it may be that his only reward:
A chance to see that he scored—
Which may not be till he meets the Lord.

And if you are fortunate
Or very importunate,
You'll have such a friend
Forever on end
With whom your life you can spend.

1966

Nancy's Wall

Nancy had a solid wall
Breached by people short and tall
Just to make the point
That anyone could flood the joint

The organizers showed their might
By traipsing through the other night
What's good for one should be good for all
And that there should be a border wall

Ms. Pelosi stood aghast
So many through her gate had passed
Worst of all what she could tell
They were ever Trumpers from their smell
She wished them all to go to hell

With power to approve a border wall
She chose instead to welcome all
Drugs and gangs no difference made
Provide the gangs fee legal aid

MS gangsters slipped right through
A border with unrestricted view
To prey upon whomever they see
To murder and rape while they stay free

The gangs moved west
Surely you can guess the rest
They scaled poor Nancy's golden gate
And put to rest her reign of hate

January 2019

State of Disunion

Hordes at the border and Dems in their caves
each settled in for immigrant waves.
Driven by smugglers and criminal knaves
the hordes crossed over to the lefts' happy raves.

The border left open to the land of the free—
all are invited, their homeland to flee.
And bring with them illness and true poverty
with no way to help build our own GDP.

Dems care not that that our taxes must pay
for unbounded willingness to let them all stay.
It matters not that some maim and slay
true citizens and cops who get in their way.

Confusion abounds in the halls of power
where most focus ire at Trump's towers of power.
Hiding behind protestations of virtue they cower
refusing to protect those who granted their power.

Dispersed though the nation new customs took hold
illegal immigrants did not meld into the fold.
They kept the customs from their land of old
but took advantage of our goodness and gold.

School rooms and hospitals were in disrepair—
learning and healthcare soon turned to despair.
Coyotes and immigrants certainly did not care
and those in power would not consider repair.

All could have been stopped by a strong border wall
but the Dems and their cronies wouldn't have that at all.
They cared not at all if the nation would fall
as long as convinced their power would not stall.

March 6, 2019

The I Factor

iPhone icons appear and disappear for no known reason,
Maybe from boredom or change of season.
Like those who appear in our lives for a time
Then disappear with neither reason nor rhyme.

A dropped call is one thing that often occurs,
A dropped friendship another whether mine or yours.
The iPhone's replaceable with little cost
But friendship is not when it has been lost.

May 31, 2019

Division of America

Folk in high places
Without names or faces
Dividing the nation
Dividing the races.

Criminal acts, too many to count
Not held to account
For treasonous actions
No charges, no doubt.

What we have is a coup
By agents untrue
Who seek to subvert
What we know to be true.

The people have spoken
Others see Trump as a token
To be taken down
With a system that's broken.

Highly placed spies
With blinds on their eyes
Leak to the press
Very well-crafted lies.

They conjure collusion
Proceed with intrusion
Of homes and offices—
Due process illusion.

Let no one be blinded
The law is one-sided
The favored skip free
All others derided.

Partisans divide the nation
Animosity their daily ration
Fueled by media bias
And provocateur oration.

The press is complicit
In foreign actions illicit
In dividing the nation
The conquest implicit.

Stand together we must
Lest our land turn to dust
United we stand, divided we fall
So in God we must trust.

September 2018

The Squad

Occasional Cortex leads a squad that spells trouble
composed of Ill Hand, Too Lib and Aryan Knot.
Reality escapes them as they live in a bubble
and none of them knows diddly squat.

They know neither history nor civics at all
but whine of America's past indiscretions.
Condemn anyone who wants a wall
then vociferously engage in misdirection.

Those who do not agree
are labeled racist and even more.
The squad is unable to see
racism is not America's core.

Slavery was ended long ago;
a war was fought to fee the slaves.
That's a fact the squad would forgo
in order to paint us all as knaves.

A contender alleges without any proof
that policing occurs in a shadow of racism.
We could regard it as kind of a spoof
except its intended to cause a great schism.

We all are tired of being accused
of all manner of nefarious things.
24/7 we all are abused;
the best we can do is ignore the stings.

Those who place these thugs into power
should be aware that they reap what they sow.
When socialists assume the levers of power
life for all will be fruitless and sour.

Freedom of speech will be gone in a flash—
the 2nd Amendment a thing of the past.
Churches and buildings will be turned into ash
and limited earnings surely won't last.

Fossil fuels and cattle will all disappear
trusting to sunlight and wind instead.
Milk and meat we once held so dear
won't matter at all once we're all dead.

July 23, 2019

Omar

Ilhan Omar says dumb things
Head coverings may be too tight.
Perhaps her intent is not to ding
But to cause division day and night.

Jews hypnotize the world, she says
And white men are worse than jihadis
I suspect I know to whom she prays
And that someone resides in Hades.

Some people did some things, she claimed
Americans themselves are to blame
Americans were killed and maimed
But to Omar it is all the same.

White men are not all racist
Black men are not all thugs
Only a few are sexist—
Only a few of them do drugs.

There are, of course, exceptions
In the course of human life
But to listen to her deceptions
Makes us fear oncoming strife.

She'd rather see America subverted
Sharia law applied throughout
The Constitution all inverted
Nonbelievers given route.

It's clear to all she hates this land
What's unclear is how she got elected.
No one asked her in-depth questions
So all her views went undetected.

Anti-Semitic and anti-white,
Anti-American to her core.
Her views sure need some oversight
Say we the mainstream: Never More!

7/26/19

COLLEGE

Meditations of a Bored Anthropology Student

In class we talk about relations
Among the sons within the nations.
All of this is, of course, related
To the way that everybody mated.

Fathers, mothers, sons and brothers
Always related to the others.
Why it is that we should care
I'll ask the teacher, if I dare.

"It's simply nice to know, you see
What ancestors might famous be
Or if perchance your blood was sired
By someone who was old and tired."

1968

Beach Bum Bradley

On the sunny sandy shore
By the shining surfing sea
There's abandoned there a cottage
By an old and twisted tree.

In that old abandoned cottage
By that old and twisted tree
Lives the ghost of Beach Bum Bradley
Who was killed in a surfing sea.

On the sunny sandy shore
By the shining surfing sea
You can see the steps of Bradley
Coming up out of the sea.

To that old abandoned cottage
By the old and twisted tree
Where the spirit of surfing seasons past
Still lingers by Bradley's sea.

1968

Mystery Girl #1

There's a girl here with blonded hair
Whose face is pretty, her figure fair.
She works downtown two blocks from me;
I wonder what her name could be?

I wonder if she'd have lunch with me
Someday when we both are free.
I don't know what she will say
But I think I'll ask her now, today.

1968

Mystery Girl #2

I can speak
With tongue in cheek
The following phrase
Which thusly says:

Your face is pretty
Your figure fair;
I'd love to touch it
But wouldn't dare.

1968

Philosophy

Philosophy appeals to me
The reason you shall quickly see:
No one can know the thoughts I think
Unless I've had too much to drink
And that's how come I get mine free.

1965

Twenty-two

Twenty and two is a cursed age
As is revealed upon this page.
The following text should well explain
Just why this age bears so much pain.

College completed, you've earned your degree
You're ready to work, but men cannot see
How they can put you in company's places
Until you've been through the Army's paces.

1968

Admonishment

You weren't prepared for class today.
You didn't quite know what to say.
The result, at which I am to wonder
Is why it is you didn't blunder.

Now we're having lunch together
forgetting past and stormy weather.
Janie's here, and so am I,
But you're the apple of my eye.

1968

Study Break

I think I should be studying.
I have a test, you know.
But it is December
And I can't remember
The things I'm s'pposed to know.

1964

Comeuppance

I like not commitments
I do not like ties
I cannot stand sentiments
And those who tell lies.

The truth shall be told
I have no reserve
If each be so bold
Let him get his deserve.

1967

FAMILY

Carrie A-Writing

There was a little girl
Who wrote in cursive style.
Each word ended with a swirl,
Each sentence with a smile.

February 27, 1989

Robert the Comic

My son is quite a joker
And he's good at playing poker.
He has card tricks and routines
That'll make 'em split their spleens!

He is smart and he is funny—
Maybe one day he'll make money
Telling jokes or doing tricks
So that people'll get their kicks.

February 27, 1989

Ode to Jay's Retirement

Farewell to those who've asked you for money;
Hello to free time to spend with your honey.
Farewell to bosses who asked you for more;
Hello to golfing from mountains to shore.

You've made all your money, so relax on your deck.
Let others get stressed over each rubber check.
From sunup to sundown just do what you will—
Why, what the heck, you're well over the hill.

So get in your camper and travel around
To faraway places where you can't be found.
Let the grass grow up under your feet
It's time to let callouses grow on your seat.

Look forward to fun, it's your time in the sun.
Know that your life's work has well been done.
Be proud of accomplishments and all you have sired.
For that's what it means to be known as "retired."

July 1990

PART II
SHORT STORIES

The Poem: An American Tragedy

The idea came to him early in a morning that he couldn't sleep: the beginning of a poem that would capture the current firestorm then in the news. He didn't publish it right away. It would stir controversy and likely offend many. He decided to put it in the public sphere by way of an anonymous blog. He chose to attribute authorship simply to "Will."

Someone, however, discovered who he was, probably by an IP trace, and here he was in a hospital bed linked to monitors and an IV. He had been brought to the hospital in a coma and had been in that state for a week before waking up. It was difficult to remember what had happened. Fragments of his memory returned a little at a time, but nothing yet that would identify the perps.

He recalled that it happened while he was hoisting the flags early in the morning, the U.S. flag on top and the Army flag underneath. His routine was to hoist them at 6:00 A.M. every morning. It was not quite light yet that October morning. With his back to the street, he sensed a presence and turned just as a huge shadow appeared out of the corner of his eye. Someone very large struck him violently. On the ground he felt kicks from at least two attackers since the kicks came from two directions.

Detectives had come to question him, but he couldn't describe anything more. He did learn from them; however, that there had been two attackers who ran when a neighbor leaving for work started the car and the lights shown on the attackers. The perps ran off and the neighbor called 911.

As he lay there, he tried to recall the attack. He had heard someone growl, "Take this, you Goddamn Republican," and "you damn Trump lover," and "you think Kavanaugh should be on the Supreme Court, you piece of…." At least he knew why he had been attacked, but not who had attacked him. He remembered that the flag was just midway up the pole when he was attacked.

He remembered a white car parked across the street, which was odd because no one ever parked there, and it just sat there for several hours with the driver inside. Days later, the same or a similar car drove slowly up and down the road next to his property, like the area was being cased. Then there were the phone calls where the caller hung up as soon as the phone was picked up. It began to seem like the assault was planned. And it was all over a poem? Over his perceived beliefs? He recalled being flipped off because he had sported the Romney/Ryan signs in the runup to the presidential election of 2012. No doubt some saw the display of the U.S. flag as an affront to those who hate America. He tried to recall the poem, but portions came only in clips…folk…divide…collusion…illusion. Then he thought of the flag left behind at half-mast as he took his last breath. He had fought in a war to preserve the right of free speech and sacrificed for that, and now he sacrificed again for his exercise of the right he had fought to protect. The offending poem, however, survived:

>Folk in high places
>Without names or faces
>Dividing the nation
>Dividing the races.
>
>Criminal acts, too many to count
>Not held to account
>For treasonous actions
>No charges, no doubt.
>
>What we have is a coup
>By agents untrue
>Who seek to subvert
>What we know to be true.
>
>The people have spoken
>Others see Trump as a token
>To be taken down
>With a system that's broken.
>
>Highly placed spies
>With blinds on their eyes
>Leak to the press
>Very well-crafted lies.
>
>They conjure collusion
>Proceed with intrusion
>Of homes and offices—
>Due process illusion.

Let no one be blinded
The law is one-sided
The favored skip free
All others derided.

Partisans divide the nation
Animosity their daily ration
Fueled by media bias
And provocateur oration.

The press is complicit
In foreign actions illicit
In dividing the nation
The conquest implicit.

Stand together we must
Lest our land turn to dust
United we stand, divided we fall
So in God we must trust.

September 2018

A Sunday Visitation

It was an extremely hot August afternoon as we stood at the way station waiting for the little train to begin its daily round of rides. The volunteer engineer steamed the little locomotive from the train barn to the way station and announced that the train would be ready in about five minutes as suddenly families with their small children swarmed where there had been no sign of life just moments before. They milled about as the engineer readied his tiny train, adding coal, adjusting the steam, and securing the all-important fare box.

"We'll start in five minutes," he announced as newcomers joined the milling families anxious to satisfy their promises of a train ride to their child-charges. Various dads scuttled their wives and children for a picture in front of the tiny caboose that stood waist-high to an average-sized adult.

"Be sure to use a flash, and stand within seven feet, to get a really good picture without shadows," said the engineer. "I used to teach photography." One by one, each of the parents adjusted the camera to comply with the engineer's instructions. "You'll get much better pictures than you've been getting," he said.

Just then, two-year-old McKenzie bolted and ran off in that fit of mischievous ecstasy so characteristic of that age group. But, as in all such breaches of decorum, it was over all too soon, in her view. And so we resumed the short wait till the engineer had readied his trusty train.

"We'll compromise," said a man from the group who had lifted his son into the last of the tiny railcars.

"He's autistic," the man announced to the group. "I'm not trying to cut ahead of anyone. He's very hyperactive, and his mother has not been disciplining him correctly. We're divorcing, and so I don't have the same degree of involvement or control. I just have him for this afternoon. He's a very smart boy, smart as a whip. He can understand, but he can't communicate."

"How old is he?" asked a woman in the group.

"He's five, but he can only speak about 25 words."

The autistic boy climbed around in the tiny train car.

"Have you found a treatment center for the boy?" asked another man.

"He's in a great school in Granite Bay. They are taking really good care of him. He should be speaking more as they work with him more."

"Well, good luck with him," added another dad.

"Yes, we wish you the best," added another mom.

"All aboard," yelled the engineer/conductor.

Everyone boarded. The engineer offered to snap pictures for anyone who wanted and worked his way down the train to snap pictures one after another.

"I'm using a flash and framing the picture within seven feet," said the engineer. "You do that, and you'll get good pictures every time. See, you got a photography lesson, too, and I'm not even charging for that."

"Thank you," everyone said, after he had taken their pictures.

The train steamed around the park on its narrow-gage track, and five minutes later everyone got off.

"Thank you," yelled several to the engineer.

The man with his autistic son mingled with some of the families, then headed to his car. He buckled his son into his seat, then ran back toward the train and picked something up off the ground. He held it up and said to anyone who could hear, "He dropped his watch. This boy is so smart. He wears two exactly alike and noticed that he only had one when he was getting into the car. He just amazes me."

"Goodbye," we smiled to him.

"Goodbye," he smiled back.

He drove away with his son, to deliver him back to the wife he was divorcing.

And the sun beat down. It was 110 degrees, and one could smell the burning coal and feel its heat 100 yards from the train that was boarding its next group of passengers.

Word Smiting

Brody slowly became aware that something was not normal. His colleagues now seemed too busy to socialize but he figured that this could just be due to stress. His profession was highly stressful, so periods of business stress was not unusual. His assignments were now the run-of-the-mill type that he had when he was first hired. In fact, his superiors were not talking to him directly at all. He thought that this might be due to a cycle of stress that was greater than usual. After all, these kinds of changes happened before, but usually resolved. This time, though, it was not resolving, and he began to feel that he was in a state of limbo. He had a gnawing feeling that something was happening behind the scenes.

As an investigative journalist, Brody had no problem seeking sources of information and asking tough and sometimes embarrassing questions. He was pragmatic, skeptical and inherently suspicious so as to confirm and reconfirm what was presented to him as fact. These qualities did not apply, however, when confronting things that affected him personally. He was like a lawyer who did not hesitate to sue on behalf of a client but would never sue on his own behalf, or like a doctor who could keenly diagnose others but hesitate to diagnose herself.

Brody had been a star journalist for a couple of decades, having won prestigious awards and even anchored a local TV news station for a while. He preferred hands-on journalism, so gave up the news anchor gig and returned to the daily grind of ferreting out the news stories. He did not think that his journalistic skills had deteriorated and so was confused about what seemed to be his diminishing status in the organization.

One of Brody's current assignments was to investigate a County Supervisor suspected of corruption. One of Brody's friends was a private investigator who helped track down information when Brody ran into a dead end. Bruce had more contacts and confidential informants than Brody ever developed and so Bruce was an important resource. Brody asked Bruce to see what he could find on the supervisor and Bruce agreed to help.

Cathy was a friend of Bruce who had worked in the office of the County Supervisors while pursuing a law degree. After getting her license, she left to join a local law firm. During lunch one day with Cathy, Bruce learned that she kept contact with her former coworkers in the County Supervisor's office and that Cathy had kept up with all the office gossip. Bruce asked if there were any rumors of corruption there. She said that there was an investigation but not into bribery or financial crimes. Instead, the investigation focused on whether a particular supervisor was colluding in efforts to undermine potential rivals through leaking to key people or publishing false allegations about the targeted individual. The supervisor did this as a matter of personal revenge or as a favor to someone else. Bruce wanted to know if Cathy knew the names of any of the people that the supervisor had targeted. She didn't, but offered to see if she could find out from any of her former colleagues.

One of Cathy's good friends, Beth, had become the supervisor's chief of staff, so Cathy invited her to lunch. As expected, there was a lot of gossip to share. Cathy wondered out loud about whether there was anything valid about rumors of corruption. Because she could not comment, Beth predictably said she didn't know about any corruption investigation. She did, however, share a funny story about how her boss let it be known that a certain investigative journalist had used the word "coon" in the past. He thought it would be funny if that journalist were to be fired for using that offensive term. When Cathy reported this to Bruce, Bruce quickly contacted Brody to let him know. Brody could not recall ever having used that term—at least not in terms of referring to a human being. He did, however, refer to the headgear he wore playing Davy Crockett as a kid to a coonskin cap, which is what it was called because it was made from raccoon skin.

Brody confirmed with Cathy and Beth what Beth had revealed. Then he wrote an op-ed that he personally delivered to his editor. He waited until the editor had finished reading the article and then asked if that was why he was being treated so cavalierly. The editor admitted that it was the reason, that management had been conducting an internal investigation and was considering firing him for use of the offensive word.

January 2019

Calizuela

Calizuela was mythical long ago, heralded as having streets paved with gold; a land of milk and honey. It was a land of opportunity. Indeed, it was the discovery of gold that drew floods of people to its rivers and streams in search of riches. They stayed; they multiplied; they created a virtual paradise. It had everything: ocean, mountains, forests, rivers and deserts. It had a mild climate and soil perfect for agriculture. Villages became towns. Towns became cities. Cities became ever larger.

People flocked to Calizuela. Its population doubled, then tripled and people kept coming to the land where success was almost guaranteed and comfortable living abounded. Laws were made to preserve this boundless country. At first, lawmakers gathered periodically to determine what rules were needed to address general concerns. They met for a while and then returned to their farms, shops or businesses to meet again when necessary. Over time the lawmakers met more frequently and eventually law making became a profession and legislating became a full-time occupation.

Calizuelans had a good life but wanted ever better lives. They petitioned the rule makers to make special laws that provided more and more benefits. When lawmakers didn't produce lavish benefits, the people elected those who would. So Calizuela built schools, highways, bridges and hospitals. It built dams. It supported farming, transportation, education and healthcare. To pay for it all, the people were taxed. As benefits increased, so did their taxes.

Over time, the demand for benefits created a class of lawmakers that devoted ever more attention to increasing benefits or creating new ones. Government came to be seen more as a candy store than a preserver of law and order. Liberalism became the face of government. The more liberal, the better. But liberalism did not account for its downside, that is, the recognition that at some point, costs outweigh the benefits.

Finally, the ultimate liberal was then elected to lead Calizuela. Free healthcare for all, he cried! Free college for everyone, he cried. The new leader charted the course for the Calizuela for the foreseeable future. Calizuela welcomed all comers however they may have arrived. Calizuela offered sanctuary to all regardless of their citizenship status. Everyone, whether or not a citizen, could get a driver's license, free healthcare and free education, including college. Non-citizens could compete for jobs with citizens. It was great, for a while, so great that people flooded to Calizuela from all over the world. Then the people realized the cost of all these benefits and that jobs had become scarce. They also noticed that their taxes had increased dramatically.

Elevation of the undocumented masses over Calizuela citizens became a fundamental tenet of the ruling class. Citizens who were arrested faced the full reach of the law. The immigrants, however, were diverted to rehabilitation services rather than incarceration, or if incarcerated, released as soon as possible. Immigrants were given preference by the government in employment and college admissions due to affirmative action. People began to get restless, then angry. Sensing an uprising of the people, the ruling class began restricting and even seizing firearms.

As people realized that Calizuela was self-destructing, they sought other places where they could live in peace and harmony, without government interference and freedom to pursue happiness and opportunity. More and more people left for better places to live. Calizuela found that it could no longer support all the benefits it had provided for its residents. The economy collapsed. Banks and stores closed. People that remained in Calizuela could not get food and starvation became rampant. People got sick and doctors and hospitals could not keep up with the demand for healthcare services. Medical supplies were exhausted. The people rioted and formed caravans to migrate to nearby countries. Calizuela devolved from richness to poverty and was consigned to the dust bin of history.

January 2019

Magical Dirt

A young man was told that there was certain dirt that had healing properties. He went in search of the healing dirt. In his search he asked countless people about where it was, but nobody seemed to know.

Then one day he met a man who said it was on some property that had been a military base. He said that he had known people that visited the site and ate dirt there. He travelled to the site as fast as he could because he needed to rejuvenate himself after a long and trying time in his chosen profession.

At the site there was a gate with a small office. A sign said that the right to enter the site required a pass and a payment of $1,000.00. He paid the guard, signed a waiver that he was too excited to read, got his pass and entered the site.

He arrived at the site, gathered a handful of dirt, hungrily put it in his mouth and washed it down with a canteen of purified water. Within seconds he felt a rush of happiness, peace and of youth. He suddenly had a lot of energy. He congratulated himself at having found what he considered the fountain of youth as it was certainly such for him. He scooped up more dirt to take with him and left the site to return home. He figured that the extra dirt could be consumed if the effects of his first dirt meal wore off.

Within a few days the young man became very ill. He was fatigued. He was losing weight rapidly. His hair was falling out. He could not eat and was in constant and debilitating pain. He lost his memory and all desire for anything. He quickly died.

As his wife was going through his papers after his death, she discovered the waiver that he had signed allowing him access to the sacred site of the magical dirt. It indeed confirmed the magical powers of the dirt but warned that eating it was at the young man's risk. It noted that the site, having been a military base at one time, contained hazardous waste that included uranium, lead, rocket fuel and other used products. The young man had sacrificed his life, and his family, for a momentary feeling of euphoria and invincibility.

March 2019

Reflections of a Psychological Garden of Eden

It has been several years now since I first met Eva. She was about four years younger than I. She was a sophomore and part-time waitress.

I was a graduate student at the University. We became close friends after meeting on campus and together we encountered a character whom neither of us shall ever forget. Our introduction to him came in a rather mysterious way. Eva, at that time, was trying to decide what she wanted to do with her life. As often happens to people in the face of such a decision, she became distressed from time to time and sometimes became mildly depressed. Such mild reactions are normal and no great cause for concern.

One of her coworkers suggested a plan of action to help her make her decision. Her friend knew of psychological tests that one could take to help determine one's vocation in life and possible aptitudes. Her friend pointed out that this was also a quick and easy way to achieve superior insight into one's self. Just by coincidence, her mother worked for a psychologist who specialized in giving such tests.

Many people do not like going to psychologists or psychiatrists because of the stigma involved. Eva was reluctant to go because of this, but her friend convinced her that there was a difference between going to a psychologist for therapy and going for mere vocational testing. Her friend argued that her own mother had sought help in this manner and was so impressed with the psychologist that "she just fell in love with him," and later became his personal secretary. The mother also had felt reluctant prior to her first psychological counselling session but had immediately seen the silliness of her fears. Eva's friend could and would arrange a special appointment through her mother to accommodate Eva. She agreed to see the doctor and an appointment was arranged.

I must jump ahead at this point in the story to describe the gist of conversations which I had with other of this doctor's patients after having met him myself. All his patients whom I could trace were unmarried women. Without exception, they all thought he was a warm, wonderful and extremely kind man. In a way it seemed that they loved him because he was so deeply interested in helping them with their problems. He was their savior, it seemed. Unmarried himself, he had a great deal of time to devote to them.

Eva had been to see the doctor twice before I became involved. Based on the results of tests administered at the first meeting he had urged her to visit him again to discuss a problem which he claimed to have discovered. He had diagnosed her as a neurotic-depressive and had intimated the possibility of eventual psychosis. He had not administered vocational aptitude tests, but personality and trait inventory tests, contrary to what she had asked for and expected. The results seemed to be inconsistent with her personality and at least gross distortions of common human moods. She was confused by this development, since she had had no serious personality problems, lost in his terminology, and naturally quite upset. She also developed doubts about the doctor, partly because of his physical appearance and partly because of a suspicion that he might be exploiting her. Since I was doing graduate work in psychology, Eva asked me to come with her on her third visit to the doctor to look at the test results and to form an independent opinion of the doctor and his findings.

I accompanied Eva on her third visit to Dr. Melpomene, who insisted on being called "Mel" by all his patients. We arrived early at his office which was in his home. Surrounded by extensive gardens, shrubbery and an abundance of fruit trees, his home may well have been in Eden, for everything was natural, growing wild, and uncared for. We were greeted by no one in the reception room until more than half an hour later.

Eventually Mel's secretary appeared, comfortably dressed in blue jeans and a knit blouse. Without acknowledging me, she handed me some paper and a pencil and asked me to draw one picture of a man and another of a woman. I explained that I was merely accompanying my friend in order to meet the good doctor. She understood why I had come but insisted that it was standard procedure for everyone to draw these figures. Mel would not be able to talk to me unless he had some insight into my personality through my drawings. She stated that Mel insisted on being very professional.

Since I had taken recent courses in psychological testing, I deliberately drew pictures which would label me as an immature, psychosexually underdeveloped pervert who had not yet resolved his Oedipus Complex. With these drawings I would soon discover Mel's level of professional competence.

When I was finished, Mel's secretary gathered my drawings and ushered us into Mel's consultation chamber. She reminded us that we were to address the doctor as "Mel," and then disappeared through a door with my drawings. She quickly returned and sat with us in silence to await the doctor's entrance.

Several minutes and much silence later, Mel made his appearance. He stood briefly in the doorway, wearing dark brown pants and a checkered orange shirt. He was a small man, bent and crippled, and old-looking. One of his legs was shorter than the other and angled away from his body. His left arm was shorter than his normal right arm. A misshapen left hand was locked downward at the wrist, gnarled and useless. With his good hand he supported himself with a gnarled and knotted cane. His head reminded me of a snake—his pointed face imbedded with two beady, furtive eyes which peered clandestinely from behind thick glasses. His mouth moved involuntarily and spasmodically, constantly contorting itself into grotesque grimaces as though he were laughing at some secret joke. A pointed black goatee complemented a snake-like countenance.

He jerked and slid into his office, took my hand into his limp, clammy one, and smiled. He looked at me with tears in his eyes, much like those of a mother welcoming her returning, wounded, war-hero son. Without speaking a word, he held my hand for a long time as though he were drawing all my knowledge of myself into his brain. He then coiled himself behind his desk and stealthily looked at my friend, then at me, back to my friend, then back to me as if trying to divine our relationship. His watchfulness reminded me of a cobra ready to strike.

I broke the silence by asking what evidence he had to support the contention that his patient was a neurotic depressive. His first statement, not a reply to my question, was an order to his secretary to make some coffee. Like an obedient and loyal servant, she left to attend to the coffee pot. Instead of directing his attention to his patient, he carefully scrutinized my drawings. He prophetically informed me that I was severely depressed, sociopathic and in need of therapy. He informed me that I hated my mother, was hostile toward women, had strong homosexual tendencies and was highly unstable.

I laughed and asked him how he could tell these things from my drawings alone, without any other supporting evidence. Not knowing of my familiarity with such tests, he pointed out that the feet of my male drawing were too small. This symbolized instability. The male figure was also clothed. This, he said, represented repressions of male sexuality and therefore indicated strong evidence of homosexual tendencies. My female drawing was also clothed. This, of course, could only mean that I had severe frustration of my carnal attitude toward women and this frustration was the cause of my very evident misogyny. My female figure also drew a hiss of satisfaction from the good doctor when he discovered that it was drawn facing left and had a sizable bust. Mel took this as a sign from the spirit of Freud, for this represented, undoubtedly, a looking backward towards, and consequently a longing for, my mother's breast. Mel was extremely excited at having found a classic textbook example of the unresolved Oedipus Complex. His test was working better than he had anticipated. He foresaw another disturbed client and income-producing visits. All I would have to do would be to pick the forbidden apple of his services and he would make me as godlike as possible.

Unknown to Mel, my test was working better than I had anticipated. I told him that I was a happy and well-adjusted person, that I was entirely able to cope with my own problems, that I had no maternal problems and no guilt feelings. Then I pointed out that I was completing my Master's degree in psychology, that I knew a great deal about this particular test, and that I had deliberately misdrawn my figures.

"Damn it," he said, slamming his good hand down on his desk, "I'm the professional here."

"Then why," I said in a joking manner, "did you miss the perversion? Could the large eyes in the male drawing imply anything but voyeurism? And is it so unusual to see men and women clothed?"

At this point a significant element of Mel's personality emerged. His mouth twisting and his eyes watering, he began drooling on his goatee and checkered orange shirt. Tearful and tender eyed, he reached out and clasped my hand saying, "I like you!" Meanwhile he slobbered even more and made no effort to conceal it. His secretary, who had returned in the meantime, also displayed watery eyes when she saw him. Mel was such a good man and such a fine doctor. After all, he was only human, and imperfectly human at that. One could scarcely blame him for such a small professional mistake as misinterpreting a test.

Having lost a potential client, Mel smiled benevolently on Eva and zeroed in on her private thoughts. After clarifying her desire for eventual marriage and family life in his mind, he asked her about her sex life. We both objected to this question as being unethical. Undaunted, he explained that marriage did not thrive on inhibition. I wondered why marriage entered so forcefully into his discussion. Then his professional point became clear. He emphatically asserted that we were incompatible and both in need of professional help in order to resolve our mutual problems before getting married.

He stated that it was best to solve as many problems as possible before marrying so that those problems which would occur after marriage would be minimal. In our case, he thought that numerous of our personal problems would have to be resolved, with his help, before we should even think about getting married. I informed Mel that we were not contemplating marriage, that he had no grounds for the statements he had made and that he had no right to make them. I suggested to Eva that we leave and we rose to our feet.

Mel apologized and begged us to stay. He didn't want us to leave with hard feelings, nor, I presumed, without paying for the visit. When we had retaken our seats, he smiled surreptitiously from one of us to the other, then brought up the point about inhibition again. This time he offered to prove his point. He directed Eva to stand up and bare her breasts, apparently assuming that if she could do so she was uninhibited and ready for marriage. In a single motion, I said this had gone too far, excused myself, grabbed Eva's hand and headed for the door. But my Latin friend shook free from my grip and turned on the doctor. She spewed forth a lingual flow of lava, thereby vindicating herself of any charge of neurotic depression, or psychic malfunction. She had discovered for herself the true intentions and motivations of the doctor of minds.

Bursting into tears at our departure, Mel began to moan and shake his pointed head. His secretary rushed protectively behind him and began to lovingly caress his head and his chest. From his twisted mouth we heard the last words we would ever hear him say: "Fools! Why won't they listen? I'm only trying to help! Oh, Mama, what's wrong?"

We had entered the serpent's world for a short time. And in that time we had been plagued by poor testing and poor advice; had met with and overcome the temptation to place any importance on Mel's services or advice; had experienced unsettling distortions of basic truths; and had exposed the pitiable and dying mind of a healer of minds. We had been indelibly marked as having been within the reach of the forbidden fruit of the serpent's advice. And leaving Eden was a pleasure rather than a pain.

1971

Shoot Up

The North Shoot Group had elected its candidate to replace Old Stump. Old Stump had lived a long life—1,753 years, until his life was cut short by a bolt of lightning the year before. Fairview seemed to be best positioned to replace the old man. He was strong, tall, was favored by the old man before the accident, and well positioned for maximum sunlight. He also had the support of other shoots in the North Group. They were not as strong, and so did not challenge Fairview. Lately, they had begun to lose their vibrant color as the sap drained from their stems, and Fairview absorbed their light and the nutrients they would have received.

As Fairview realized that he was chosen/destined to succeed Old Stump, he began to change. He came to believe that he was superior to the other shoots, so young, tender and scraggly, and that he was favored by the sun, the water, the wind, and the spirits of the surrounding forest. He saw himself growing fast and towering above all the trees of the forest.

As so often is the case when one declares himself a leader and asserts authority, no matter how ill prepared for leadership, sycophants accept the declaration of authority and lend their efforts toward supporting the self-declared king of the hill. They never consider that they may be more than they already are, that they might reach to greater heights, or provide better for themselves or their neighbors than their self-declared leader. And so it was with Fairview and his cousins.

Fairview began thinking of himself as the Great Stump. In his mind, he had no competition. He was heir to Old Stump by fiat of the Divine Forest Spirit. He was entitled to gather solely for his own growth all nutrients—that it was inevitable that others would die so that he could thrive. Survival was his by divine right. On the North Side, Fairview grew strong while his brothers, cousins and North Group neighbors slowly perished.

On the south side of Old Stump there emerged several young shoots. On the south side there was not as much sunlight. It was moist, and darker than on the north side. None of the young shoots showed much promise of leadership or primacy, but they knew that not all of them could survive by competing for the nutrients in the limited space that they shared. Clea was an enterprising shoot and put her mind to work. She thought that if each of her fellow shoots contributed some of their remaining energy to one shoot, that shoot could grow toward the sun. They agreed, and Moss, the tallest shoot so far, was assigned to grow toward the light as fast as he could. He grew and as he took in sunlight, he shared it with his fellow shoots so that finally, all survived. Eventually, the south shoots outgrew Fairview, but since Fairview was on the far side, the southerners could not reach out to help him and he faded away.

Opportunity Lost

Jamie already had a difficult life. She was born by C-section prematurely at eight months when her mother was injured in a car accident. The doctors thought that the mother would die since her injuries were so bad. Her mother survived but was paralyzed and confined to a wheelchair. She was not able to be a mother to Jamie. To make matters worse, Jamie had Down Syndrome (DS) that caused her many difficulties. She had difficulty learning to speak. She needed special education classes. There were difficulties socializing with kids other than those with DS.

There was no father in Jamie's life. Her Aunt Becky was a single mom of Tom, a boy slightly older than Jamie. Becky took Jamie to live in her house and did her best to raise Jamie. Tom and Jamie were close. Becky and Tom were the constants in Jamie's life. Tom grew tall and was a good athlete. He had taught Jamie to catch a ball and often played catch with her when they were young. Tom liked basketball and was on his high school's basketball team in his freshman year. One day during practice Tom collapsed and died. No one knew that he had a heart problem. Jamie was inconsolable. Without Tom her life had no meaning. Her life could not get any worse.

Aunt Becky did her best to see that Jamie learned what she needed to survive in the world. She noticed that Jamie had talent working with her hands. She learned to color within the lines. She liked to draw, though the drawings were quite rough. She was coordinated enough to catch balls that Tom threw to her. When Jamie was encouraged to help with painting a room, she preferred using a small brush and did quite well, even in the difficult spots like corners and eves. In short, Jamie liked to work with her hands. When working with her hands, she could concentrate for long periods of time. It was something she enjoyed, and it took her mind off her loneliness after Tom died.

Becky realized that Jamie would need to find work where she would use her hands. Something routine could be ideal and something she could do at her own pace. She realized that most jobs were paced and detailed. Sorting products on an assembly line would not work, nor would detail work like electronics assembly. Also, the work would need to be done at home as Jackie would never be able to drive. In searching for the right kind of job, Becky learned of an occupation called esthetician. She learned that it took up to 1,000 hours of training, that full-time school can take four to six months to complete, and that part-time school can take up to 9 to 12 months. The cost could be as much as $12,000.00 depending on the type of school. Becky had little money to spare but was determined to see if Jamie could be trained as an esthetician. She enrolled Jamie in a local school. Luckily, Jamie did well during that training and became a certified esthetician after more than a year of training and before she was 20 years old. Becky helped get Jamie a business license and to establish advertising for providing the service in her home.

Jamie got a couple of clients in the first month that she opened her waxing business. With advertising and word-of-mouth recommendations, she got more customers the next months and even more after that. She was good at waxing and it was a plus that she had DS because she was gentle and non-threatening. Her customers were very comfortable with her. Of course, all her customers were women. One day, however, a man showed up without an appointment and asked for her services. Becky answered the door and told the man that services were for women only. The man said he identified himself as a female and demanded that he be waxed. Becky explained that the training for estheticians did not address male waxing and that Jamie was trained and certified for services only to women. With that she bid the man farewell and closed the door.

Weeks later, Becky and Jamie were served with a complaint. The man had filed a civil rights complaint alleging discrimination in the administration of esthetician services. Becky was devastated and Jamie did not understand what was happening. Becky didn't have the money to hire a lawyer. She decided to handle the matter as best she could by herself. She filed an answer to the complaint and hoped for the best. Before the matter was to be heard in court, the plaintiff offered to withdraw his complaint if Becky or Jamie paid him $3000.00. Becky declined, both on principle and lack of money.

The case was heard by a judge who, after listening to both sides, ordered that esthetician services be provided to the plaintiff or for the business to be closed. Becky was stunned. She had argued that estheticians were not trained to wax males and certainly were not certified for waxing males. She argued that providing such a service to the plaintiff could result in a sexual assault claim if the plaintiff or other male thought that there had been any inappropriate touching of the genitals. Her arguments fell on deaf ears. The judge had been persuaded to believe that the simple self-identification of a man as a female governs how that man should be treated.

Becky's only recourse was to close the business. When there were no more customers, Jamie wondered what she had done wrong. She became depressed and never recovered.

8/4/19

Red Flag

Joe's neighbor was always complaining about something. Lately his neighbor, McNally, complained about the house he was building for his aging parents. McNally complained to the county housing commission whenever he thought of something being wrong with the construction: The house was too close to the street or to the fence dividing Joe's and McNally's properties. He complained about the noise and the dust. McNally, for whatever reason, did not like Joe.

Over the past few years, the neighborhood had changed. Once rural, housing developments sprang up, including apartment complexes. Traffic increased. Burglaries were on the rise. In the past couple of years, the epidemic of homelessness started encroaching on this once rural community. Illegal camping became common along the river, the creeks and the bike trails. Homeless tents were even erected on vacant properties.

When it became apparent that drug transactions were occurring and gangs started infiltrating the community, Joe figured it was time to think about his ability to defend his family and his property. He bought a couple of revolvers, a rifle and a shotgun. He took a gun safety course and signed up with a firearms practice facility. Joe had never had a problem with the law. He was a CPA and was highly respected by his clients, his church and the community. Joe had served his country in combat and never regretted his service despite having been wounded.

Joe's eight-year-old son, Josh, was playing with a friend one day when McNally was tending to some plants in his front yard. The boys bantered with each other as boys do and Josh bragged about his dad having guns in case somebody ever tried to break into their home. Josh said his dad would blast an intruder to smithereens. McNally heard this conversation. Based on what he heard, he concluded that Joe was dangerous and posed a threat to the neighborhood.

The County had adopted a red flag law. McNally filed a complaint with the County the next day, as soon as the County building opened for business. He signed a complaint form saying that his neighbor had threatened to kill and posed a threat to him and to the community. The very next day police served Joe with a warrant to take his guns. Joe was stunned. Not wanting to appear to resist the police by claiming his Second Amendment rights, Joe gave his guns to the police.

Under the Red Flag Law, Joe was entitled to a court hearing about his guns being confiscated. His hearing was scheduled for the following month. Joe set about gathering statements from family, friends and clients as to his character, and asked some of them to testify on his behalf. All readily agreed because Joe was an outstanding citizen who had never even spoke unkindly about anyone, let alone ever having been physically aggressive.

A couple of weeks later, armed burglars entered Joe's home in the middle of the night. The burglars had silenced the dogs with sedative-filled dog food so that they could not alert the family with barking. Joe, however, was not asleep because he was worrying about his pending court hearing. He heard the burglars. He quickly dialed 911 to report the burglary and then looked for something he could use to deal with the burglars. The only things he had that could be used as a weapon were a baseball bat and a hunting knife. He woke his wife and his two sons and told them to go out onto the roof and quietly hide themselves. But as they were preparing to do that, a burglar appeared at the bedroom door. Joe charged the burglar with his bat and knife in hand, but was shot and killed. Joe's wife and sons were also killed because they could identify the burglar.

Joe's clients, fellow parishioners and the community mourned the loss of Joe and his family. Joe's coffin was dressed in the flag of red, white and blue. McNally, alone, did not mourn or attend the funerals; and the red in the flag on Joe's coffin did not, in any way, serve as a tribute to the Red Flag Law.

8/29/19

PART III
ESSAYS

Abortion Paradigms

We live in an age in which animal rights appear more important than the rights of fetuses and newborn babies. Animals are given special legal protections. Killing or harming a pet will earn the malfeasor jail time. Entire species are protected by law from human activity that would impair their existence. Violation of rules and regulations earn hefty fines. Environmental studies are required for construction permits. Following the rules can take years. Costs for pursuing permits and costs engendered by delays mount steadily. There can be no doubt that our society places a great deal of emphasis on sustaining and preserving the animal and environmental kingdoms in the name of protecting animal and insect species.

The same is not true for human life. For decades laws sanctioning abortion of human fetuses have devolved. Originally, in the early 1970s, abortion was allowed but limited to the first three months of pregnancy and in circumstances where the health of the mother was at stake. The law allowing abortion was intended for rare circumstances. In recent times, several states have enacted or proposed laws that allow abortion up to birth. Virginia almost adopted a law allowing for post-birth annihilation of a live human being.

In the last trimester of fetal development, and even earlier, a fetus can survive outside the womb. There can be no doubt that a fully formed fetus is a human being, complete with heartbeat and a working alimentary system. The location of a living being in America should make no difference, whether in or out of the womb. Any living human born in America is automatically a citizen of the United States with the constitutional protection. Pursuant to the *Declaration of Independence*, each citizen is entitled to life, liberty and the pursuit of happiness. Animals, on the contrary, have no citizenship rights or constitutional protections but are nonetheless given advanced status in our society.

Some legislators and those devoted to the right of a woman to choose seem to think of womb dwellers and even born individuals as somehow not quite human and not quite entitled to life unless the mother thinks otherwise. Basically, our society gives women and their doctors a license to kill. Is not a child outside the womb a human being entitled to due process and the protections of society? Is a fully formed individual in the womb that is capable of living outside the womb not a human being entitled to legal protections? Federal law provides for birthright citizenship for babies born on United States soil by women not legally present in the United States. Would not the concept of birthright citizenship apply to newborns of U.S. citizens? Yet the outcry for killing or harming animals is so loud as to drown out any concept of fairness for humans to be considered at least as being on a par with animals. Killing newborn puppies can result in arrest and incarceration, but killing a newborn human would be condoned by law in some jurisdictions and may well become the new normal for dealing with unwanted newborn babies and viable fetuses.

The mindset involved here is troublesome. Human beings are part of the animal kingdom, yet humans are seen, at least in their beginning stages, as less valuable than pets. The solution is actually quite simple. We could start thinking of babies, and potential babies, as pets and give them the same status and rights that we provide to the animal kingdom. It's sad to think that fetuses and babies need to be upgraded in status to that of pets.

Since a newborn is a citizen with all rights of citizenship, protection should be provided to a newborn targeted for extinction with a protection order that would be automatically stayed until such time as the child could be educated enough to understand the document affecting his or her life. The same should be true for a viable fetus. A child targeted for extinction should have the same rights of appeal as afforded to criminals that have been sentenced to death. After all, a fetus or a newborn has done nothing to deserve a death sentence other than to have been conceived or born through no fault of its own. The mindset needs to change and thinking of viable fetuses and babies as pets may help them to be seen as living beings entitled to comfort, care and protection. If it takes considering newborns or womb dwellers as pets, or as comfort animals, so be it.

Abuse

My long-term memory goes back to age two. I remember trying to figure out how people turned, which was something that intrigued me at the time. On a couple of Sundays I looked out our front window to the church that sat across the street from our house. I was determined to unlock the secret of how people turned. On the second Sunday of my observations, I watched carefully as a woman came out of the church to her car that was parked in front. I noticed that to effect a turn, she changed direction with her left leg as she was about to turn left. And so I figured out how people turned. A little older, around the age of four, I knew that there was a difference between men and women, and I tried mightily to figure out the difference. With a lot of thought, I came pretty close to what I actually learned much later in life. I remember most things that occurred in my life, including instances of clergy abuse.

In my case, it was rather mild in terms of two events that I remember. The first occurred in a Catholic kindergarten in St. Louis. I was five years old. One very cold winter day, we boys trooped in and the nun had us line up and stand on benches in an L-shaped hallway. She told us that we needed to unzip our pants so she could make sure our private part had not been frozen, explaining that it was okay because she had brothers. It didn't make sense, but who were we to question authority and each of us unzipped for the "inspection." Later in life, as a young adult, a priest kissed me in trying to make a pass. I simply ignored it, but never forgot. It was very uncomfortable. These two instances were minor compared to what is reported as happening to others.

It occurs to me now that there may have been another instance of abuse. When I was four years old my mom traveled east with me to escape from a threat by my dad to take custody of me. On the way east we stopped at various points for my mom to secure lodging or visit relatives. One such stop was in Malden, Missouri, where my mom had arranged to be housekeeper for a priest who had moved there from our hometown. My long-term memory has been good throughout my life. However, I remember going up the steps to the rectory, but remember absolutely nothing for the two weeks that we were there. I believed that the priest summarily fired my mom and heard that he had a really bad temper and complained that she could no nothing right. I was told that he was not happy with a cake she made and had thrown it across the kitchen and that was what caused her to be fired.

Because those two weeks are a complete blank in my mind, I'm wondering now if I was the object of some abuse that I unconsciously blocked out and that the explanations for why we had to leave were invented to protect me. I wouldn't be surprised because my mom was very protective of me.

In St. Louis, my uncle's in-laws kindly took us in. While there I escaped what looked to be a near instance of physical abuse. I had developed a case of measles and was confined in an upstairs bedroom for several days. One day when I finally felt better, I ventured downstairs to see if I could get something to eat and drink. The steps were very narrow. I was a little lightheaded from being in bed for several days and I fell slightly into the stove at the bottom of the stairs. The man of the house was the only one there because his wife and my mom worked during the day. When he saw that I had stumbled, he became angry and pulled off his belt, saying, "I'll show you to hit the stove." Although still a bit woozy, I dashed upstairs, closed the bedroom door and hoped he would not come after me. Thankfully he didn't. I told my mom what had happened and we left shortly thereafter.

I guess there was a milder form of abuse involving my dad. When I was three years old, my dad arranged for a trip with my mom and me to Seaside, Oregon. When we got into his car, he ordered me to sit in the back and be quiet. I didn't like that at all. When we got to Seaside, he pulled my trike out of the trunk, said to follow him and my mom far behind while they walked and talked. I didn't like that either and I decided that I did not like him. The talk didn't last long because after a walk around a short block we got back in the car and drove back in total silence. My guess was that the talk didn't go well.

A few months later my dad arranged for me to spend a Sunday afternoon with him. He picked me up and took me to his home. There he told me to go out in the backyard and play. A swing set was all there was. He left me alone and made no contact until it was time to return me home. It was the worst day of my life. I felt totally abandoned. The only saving factor was that on the way out, an aunt had come home with her boyfriend and they were sitting in the front room. My aunt was glad to see me and she made me feel a lot better. It was after that incident that my mom decided to move away. Maybe he simply didn't know how to be a dad, but regardless, I never wanted to see him again.

November 2018

Angel of God

Angel of God, my guardian dear,
To whom God's love commits me here,
Ever this day be at my side,
To light and guard, to rule and guide.
Amen.[1]

Introduction
Life is full of cues about what is to come. The trick is to pay attention and try to understand the clues and the ensuing life event. The attitude I have brought to my life is going with the flow. Each of us has interests and aptitudes that pull us in certain directions. Where these interests and aptitudes come from is perhaps genetic, inspired, learned or a combination thereof. At any rate, they are what drive our existence and paying attention to them is extremely important but not completely determinative. There are also less tangible factors and influences. Unplanned incidents and events become the story of our life.

In my life there have been many miracles. I have no doubt that they shaped who I became, and I believe that they led me to follow the path that was set out for me, not necessarily the path I chose for myself. If we look back on life, we see that there were sometimes little events that change the course of life. In my life there were several events that determined who and what I became.

Woman on the Prescott Bus
The first event that I can recall that had supernatural overtones happened when I was about three years old. My grandmother took me to downtown Portland for some shopping and sightseeing. On the way back, as the bus travelled down Prescott Street toward our house an extraordinary even occurred. It was empty except for my grandmother and me, the driver, and a woman. We were at the front of the bus. I sat on the seat behind the driver, the one facing the aisle. My grandmother was in the first seat facing forward. Across from me was a pretty woman dressed in a white skirt with a matching jacket. She smiled at me.

A few minutes before our stop, my grandmother and the woman in white started talking. The woman in white commented what a fine-looking boy I

---
[1] This is a prayer that I learned and recited in my childhood.

was. My grandma said thank you to the woman and volunteered that my parents were separated and going through a divorce. The woman then said, "That is too bad. Children of broken homes always grow up bad." I was happy up to that point. But the woman predicting a bad future for me was disturbing. I didn't say anything, but in my head I said, "I'll show you! I will grow up to be good." I took it as a challenge. Looking back to that episode, proving the woman wrong became my life goal.

Perhaps it was because I had a genetic nature of a fighter. I don't know. I just know that I never backed down from a challenge. That woman's challenge became a driving force in my life. It is the one thing from that day that has stood out in my mind. Other details of that day did not stick and I do not remember them. But I can never forget what that woman said or the details of that conversation. The woman in white was in my life for only a few moments in time, but those few moments dictated the course of my life. I spent the rest of it doing my best to prove her wrong. I've wondered, of course, if she was an angel who appeared briefly in human form charged with kickstarting my life down a preordained road. I don't know, but would not be surprised. There were just too many situations in my life that defy a human explanation. I think of them as interventions, this being the first one that I recall.

Darting Across 14th Avenue

The next intervention when I was seven years old saved me from my own thoughtlessness, stupidity actually. My favorite activity was riding my bike all over the neighborhood in Sacramento. The neighborhood was quiet and did not have a lot of car traffic. It was familiar, and safe. Familiar and safe became boring after a while so I ventured without thinking. Not far from my neighborhood was 14th Avenue, a busy thoroughfare. I decided to explore the neighborhood across 14th. I pedaled fast and darted across 14th without looking for traffic either way. My focus was solely on getting across 14th Avenue to see what was on the other side. Once across I realized how lucky I was and how stupid I was not to have looked for traffic. There was heavy traffic in both directions when I looked back.

I read this now as a sign that someone was looking out for me. Timing was everything in terms of crossing that street, and I had paid absolutely no attention to timing. Someone or something saved me from injury or death. When I crossed back over, I used my head and made sure the street was clear before crossing. That intervention taught me to think about what I'm doing, to be cautious and to plan. Was it luck, or was it intervention? I don't know, but I like to think that someone or something was watching out for me so that my life could continue and have meaning.

Runaway Car

I became convinced that someone was watching out for me and that it was a supernatural being that I thought of as an angel. We had moved to a different part of town. I was ten years old. I was walking on a main street near my home just before the street began an upward slope. On the next block there was a parallel access road serving homes set back from the main street. As I was walking toward that access road, a car that had been parked in front of one of the houses on the frontage road started rolling downhill. I did not notice it until it was about 100 feet from me and gathering speed. I was shocked and totally frozen. I could not move. I thought about jumping out of the way, but my body would not move. It was like I was frozen in time. Then, inexplicably, the car stopped within inches. I could not then, and cannot now, understand how I was spared in human terms. The only explanation is that there was a supernatural intervention. I believed, and continue to believe, that I have a guardian angel—a being appointed by God to keep me out of trouble so that I can do what I was destined to do.

Essay on St. Brendan the Navigator

I recall being in the 4th grade and there being a writing contest. Students throughout California were encouraged to write and submit an essay. I don't recall why, but I chose to write about St. Brendan the Navigator. For some reason I devoted quite a bit of time on it with reading about him and writing the essay. In the 1950s there were no computers and we did not have a typewriter, so I had to write it by hand. My mom and my aunt thought handwriting was very important and made me write it over and over until the handwriting was perfect. I also think that there was some guidance by my guardian angel to keep me focus and interested. The effort paid off as I won the statewide competition. This exercise taught me that writing was an art to be pursued and that perseverance was important to achieving goals. Someone or something besides my mom and my aunt may have been influencing me.

Another Stranger

At age 14 I had decided to be a priest and had entered the seminary. My best friend had also entered the same seminary. During one holiday vacation, my friend and I planned to go downtown to look around. We waited for a bus at a bus stop in a shopping village. As we stood there, a man appeared seemingly out of nowhere, although he may have been standing unnoticed. He came up to me and said, "You're going to be a priest, aren't you?" I turned to my friend to say, "Did you hear that?" When I turned back to the man he was not there. We were in a vacant parking lot and the nearest building was 50 yards away. There was no sign of the gentleman. He simply appeared and disappeared. I chalked it up to the same type of experience as the woman on the bus who said I would never amount to anything. I took it as a sign that I was on the right path, although I ultimately did not follow that path.

Eel River Crossing

In 1961 I was attending the seminary that was then located in Rio Dell, California. One day in the spring of that year some of my classmates and I went down to the Eel River. To this day, I don't know why, but a classmate and I decided to swim across the river. The only stroke I knew was the crawl and even then I was not good at it. Halfway across the river I was out of breath and gasping for air. Stopping was not an option so I kept going, although in panic mode, and made it to the other side. Upon reaching the shore we crawled into the mud panting and exhausted. It took about an hour to recover, and then we had to decide how to get back. The town and the bridge were upstream maybe a mile or more. Barefooted and cold it didn't seem like a good option. The other option was to swim back and that's what we did. The swim back was just as bad. I gasped and panicked halfway across, but we made it. I always felt afterward that someone was looking out for me.

Rocket Explosion at Long Binh, Vietnam

The Long Binh base was a target for the Viet Cong in 1969, the year I was there. We were attacked nightly. The Army hired locals to fill jobs such as hooch cleaners, waste burners, barbers, and more. They worked for the Army during the day, but some were Viet Cong who participated in the night attacks on the base. Sometimes they fired rockets, usually at night, but sometimes during the day. One day after lunch I was walking from the mess hall when I heard an incoming rocket that seemed to be coming pretty close to my location. I dove to one side of a small berm and the rocket landed on the other side of the berm. The berm protected me from the effects of the blast. I was protected again by divine intervention as I had mere seconds to decide which side of the berm to dive to.

Life Mission

I had a lot of plans for what I wanted to do in life, like being a priest, a doctor, or a psychologist. I worked toward each in turn and encountered obstacles with each. Near the end of my tour of duty in the Army I applied to the University of Portland with the idea of becoming a counseling psychologist but had to wait a year before I could enroll. In the meantime, simply for the fun of the experience, I took the law school entrance exam. I never thought I could actually be a lawyer and the competition in the exam process left me feeling totally unqualified. However, I passed and was accepted into law school. With the very first class I was hooked on the law and threw myself into it wholeheartedly. I attended night school because I had to work. Again, I attribute the experiences and decisions that led to this profession to my guardian angel.

Pieces of My Life Puzzle

I was guided to an interview for a job with the State of California where I was hired into a group of analysts who researched and wrote the *Dictionary of Occupational Titles*. This was a program directed by the Federal Department of Labor. I spent my law school years working on that book. Little did I know that was part of the Divine Plan for me. The next part if the Divine Plan was for me to get experience in litigating disability cases. I ended up working for a retirement system, where I handled hundreds of disability retirement cases. After some years there, I left and started a private practice devoted to representing disabled people, which turned out to be my true-life goal. Much of my practice involved representing disabled people claiming Social Security disability benefits. I believe I was guided in my academic career to the legal profession that turned out to be what I was destined to do. I spent my career helping sick and injured people get disability benefits. As it turned out, SSA used the *Dictionary of Occupational Titles* to determine whether there was or was not any work that a disabled person could do. Long story short, everything I did led to a very rewarding career that would not have occurred without there having been a divine plan that kept leading me in the right direction. Was that mere coincidence or divine intervention? I suspect the latter explanation.

Location of Father

After I married and had started a family, I thought that I should try to contact my dad so that he would know that he had grandchildren and so that they could get to know him. I had no idea how to get in touch with him and all attempts to locate him did not work. In or around 1979 he got a speeding ticket while driving through California. Somehow that citation came to the attention of a family member and that provided me with the information I used to contact him. He was very happy to meet me and my family, and that would not have occurred, I believe, but for his angel guiding him to a speeding ticket and my angel getting the information to me. Mere coincidence is astronomically impossible.

Salvage from Rogue River

On one family vacation we stayed at a park alongside the Rogue River in Oregon. Rafting trips could be arranged in Grants Pass with an option of using a kayak rather than floating on a raft with lots of other adventurers. My son and I chose to kayak. With only brief instructions we set out, only to find the kayaks unmanageable. They were blowups rather than solid kayaks. We were told to avoid rocks and were able to do that until I couldn't avoid one. In mere moments I was scraping the bottom of the river and could not even see daylight. I held what little breath I had until my lungs about burst. My life jacket popped me out of the river at the point where I didn't think I could hold my breath any longer. My son paddled furiously to help me.

The fact that I survived I again attribute to my guardian angel. Thinking back, I could have been trapped by debris and drowned, but there was an intervention. My guardian angel again came to my rescue so that I could carry out the divine plan that God had for me.

The Bear

In the mid-1970s I decided to take a hike in Sequoia National Park. As I was hiking up a hill I encountered a bear coming down the hill. We both stopped about 20 yards apart. The bear stood up on its hind legs and I stood completely still. We stared at each other for several moments. Once the bear saw that I was not a threat, he bounded off the trail to the left. I don't know to this day why I reacted as I did, except to attribute it to another intervention by my guardian angel. I had no experience hiking and no education about how to deal with wildlife. Divine intervention is the only reasonable explanation.

Medical Interventions

Diaphragmatic Hernia

In 1977 my son was born with a diaphragmatic hernia. A sharp nurse noticed his labored breathing and saw that it was an emergency situation. He was quickly diagnosed. One of only ten surgeons that performed repair of such hernias on babies practiced in nearby Los Angeles. He was summoned to perform the emergency surgery and so my son was saved. Here I suspect that several angels were involved, my son's, the nurse's, and the doctor's.

Lymphoma

Having served in Vietnam, Agent Orange had a role in my life. In 1990 a very savvy nurse suspected that I had non-Hodgkin's lymphoma. Because of the nurse's suspicion and quick intervention, the lymphoma was caught at its first stage. Following surgery and chemotherapy, I was cured. The intervention of the nurse was, in turn, an intervention by my guardian angel.

Bar Exam

After law school I had to pass the state bar in order to practice law. This was scheduled in late February 1977. My son had been born a month earlier and underwent emergency surgery shortly after birth and hospitalized through February. Accordingly, I could not study for the exam and almost chose to defer taking it. The decision to take the exam was at the last minute. Not only had I not studied, but my electric typewriter malfunctioned and all rental typewriters were all rented out. I had typed all my exams throughout law school and so had no confidence in writing an exam by hand. Fortunately, a coworker loaned me an old manual typewriter to use for the exam. Despite all the obstacles, I passed the exam. Again, I attribute the outcome to the help of my angel to overcome each obstacle. The earlier lesson about perseverance paid off.

Family

My angel also had a hand in the creation of my family. My ex-wife introduced me to my current wife, a quite unusual event. This, too, was at divine direction and intervention, that is, the termination of one relationship and the introduction to another. These two events turned out to be a godsend because what we have built in terms of a family is a true blessing. Looking at my children and grandchildren is a source of great pride and so I thank my guardian angel, and God, for my wife and my family. I couldn't be more proud.

Book Selections

I have always enjoyed reading and so have visited bookstores a lot. One thing that occurs repeatedly is that some force guides my attention to a particular book among several on a shelf to which I've paid little or no attention. The books to which I have been guided have brought necessary understandings to my life and have shaped my thinking in ways that have helped me immensely. The force guiding me to these books is my guardian angel.

    I thank God for sending us angels, and I'm particularly thankful for mine. This angel has performed magnificently, guiding me through the plan that God has for me and intervening to keep me out of the way of myself and my mistakes.

December 2018

Choosing Freedom

In the year 2019 we are living in a version of George Orwell's *1984*. Words are redefined to suit the narrator or discarded altogether. Gender no longer distinguishes between male and female but has proliferated into dozens of iterations and combinations that were never contemplated until recently.

Imprinting is the life blood of our cultural existence. The culture into which we are born dictates how we view the world. If I'm born into a Catholic family, I grow up attending Mass, Catholic schools and praying in the language of Catholicism. If I am born into a Jewish family, I grow up learning the Torah, attending a Synagogue and having a Bar Mitzva. If I am born Muslim, I pray five times each day using a prayer rug and facing Mecca. If I am born into a family of atheists, I grow up believing that God does not exist. In every case, I believe, or assume, that my culture is the true culture and that other cultures are either wrongheaded or inferior. We are indoctrinated by our culture and our mind set is sculpted in mental and emotional concrete. The way we conduct our lives is dictated by the belief system into which we are born. It is in this sense that we are not free.

Freedom exists within a framework of choice. Choice, in turn, depends on investigating and carefully considering the underlying principles upon which our inbred culture is founded. We must ask whether each principle of our culture is solidly grounded, whether it is rational, and whether it is relevant. It necessarily follows that one must step away from one's inbred culture to look objectively at its underpinnings. That is difficult to do if the culture guarantees an eternity of hellfire for one so foolish as to question the culture's underpinning, i.e. dogmas, proclamations of God, Jesus, Allah, Mohammed, Moses or any of the plethora of divine or semi-diving personages.

Freedom is a state of mind, literally. The first step toward freedom is to choose to mentally separate from one's culture in order to seek unbiased truths. This is fundamentally necessary to question the rationality of beliefs. One must question whether a precept makes sense, whether its purpose was rational and relevant, or political and manipulative. One must assess what the precept was intended to accomplish among peoples or flocks that had little or no education. One must question if a precept would be similarly established for those with educated minds. One must assess whether a precept has stagnated or evolved over time. Ultimately one must determine if the precept was correct. Science, for example, debunked the precept that the sun revolved around the earth. Galileo was condemned by the Church for daring to contend that the reverse was true. Centuries later his theory was proved to be correct.

Organizations, cultures and cults are creations of man. Mankind is not infallible. Mistakes are the rule, not an exception to the endeavors of mankind. Discoveries and inventions are the product of making and correcting mistakes. There would be little if any progress without mistakes. Freedom ensues from adjusting from mistakes and assessment of beliefs.

May 5, 2019

Coping with Adversity

Early in life I was informed that God tests us during our lives but that He never gives us a challenge that we could not overcome. The corollary precepts were that every cloud has a silver lining and that whenever a door closes, another opens. I have found these precepts to be true both from my own experiences and the experiences of others.

John McCain provides one such example. He endured more than five years of hardships and challenges as a prisoner of war after being captured by the Viet Cong. By all accounts he was treated miserably and sustained great damage to his body. After his release and return to America, he became a political legend, based in part on his service to his country and his status as a POW. In that capacity he did a great deal of good for his nation when he could have simply accepted his disability and lived a life of ease. He overcame serious challenges and entered the new door that had been open to him.

John F. Kennedy also served during war time accomplishing life-threatening feats. After the loss of his PT boat he swam a great distance to shore and managed to save crew members in the process. After his service he faced daunting physical challenges including a broken back and Addison's disease. He could have gone on disability and given up. He chose instead to enter politics, ultimately being elected to the highest office in the land, the Presidency of the United States. He overcame substantial obstacles placed in his way in order to fulfill his destiny. Sadly, he gave his life for his service to his country.

Yet another example is my own. I served in Vietnam at the height of the Vietnam War. Fallout from that experience included multiple problems due to contact with Agent Orange. The Vietnam experience was certainly an obstacle placed in my way as one of God's tests. However, that experience paved the way for me to use the GI Bill to complete my education which inured to the advantage of my family and me. Effects of Agent Orange, however, posed several health problems for me and my family.

Among those effects, in order of their occurrence, several of my wife's miscarriages, the birth of our son with a life-threatening diaphragmatic hernia, my challenge with non-Hodgkin's lymphoma and coronary artery disease, and birth of a grandson with Down Syndrome. Despite these consequences of voluntary military service I am nevertheless grateful for the obstacles placed in my way. They tell me that God was interested in my life by presenting challenges that He hoped I would overcome. I hope that I have not disappointed.

November 2018

Letting Go and Adapting to Change

I was born into a staunch Irish-Catholic family, complete with Catholic schools and unfailing attendance at Sunday Mass. Grandpa walked to church every day. We prayed the rosary every evening without fail. Grandpa compulsively but silently prayed the rosary every waking moment. Priests were frequent guests in our home, even for cards on Sunday afternoons. I was conditioned in the Catholic tradition and so it was inevitable that I wanted to be a priest. So, at age 14 I started down that path having entered the seminary.

The education was really good and the experience was fun and rewarding in the early years. As my mind developed I started noticing things that did not make sense. My skeptical nature emerged, and I started thinking things through and questioning basic assumptions. For me, things had to make sense. The purpose of the seminary was to train future priests to represent church teachings to their future flocks. The doctrines we were to teach and enforce were firm and unchangeable. As we learned these doctrines in depth, more and more questions arose. We were encouraged to accept the teachings on faith that they were true. Questioning doctrine was taboo and I learned that the uncomfortable way.

In a religion class on the Ten Commandments there was an in-depth session on the fifth commandment. It was more than just about killing. The essence of the lesson was that it included harming others or oneself. My skepticism kicked in and so I raised my hand to ask a question: "If the Church canonizes people who flagellate themselves, or throw themselves into thorny bushes, or sleep on nails to purge their minds of impure thoughts, how is that not a violation of the commandment against harming oneself?" That one question sealed my fate. The teacher's whole head turned bright red. He declined to answer the question. From that moment on I became an unworthy candidate for the priesthood. The seminary priests knew it, and I knew it. I left the seminary and the priesthood behind at the end of that academic year. It was best that I leave because I knew I could not promote the party line were I to become the spiritual adviser to unsuspecting Catholics as a priest.

The seminary experience taught me to think for myself. It is too easy to blindly accept what we are told or taught by others. Without questioning anything, intellectual development fails to evolve. Just because something is touted as true doesn't make it so. Blind acceptance is akin to imprinting behavior.

People, like baby ducklings, mimic the behavior of their mothers. In Pavlovian or imprinting terms, when applied to children, they never deviate from what they learned at their parents' knees. Once a Catholic or Protestant—always a Catholic or a Protestant. Or being born into a particular political party, never thinking to change that affiliation. Thinking can be quite uncomfortable for many and so basic assumptions remain unchallenged and therefor all controlling.

After leaving the seminary I eventually left my Catholicism behind, too, but not without a lot of researching and thinking through more issues than I can recall. In the end, weighing the pros and cons, I simply abandoned my pre-conditioned Catholicism. In reality, I abandoned man-controlled religion altogether in favor of a one-on-one connection with God and the natural and supernatural order of things. I have marched to the beat of my own drummer.

Accepting doctrine of whatever sort and not questioning it leads to the inability to note and respond to change. Change is fundamental in all of nature. Growth and aging involve change. Evolution involves change. Civilization and nature are in a constant state of flux. Religion and politics are not exempted from change. Not accepting the reality of change is self-limiting. The religion of my youth is not the same. It used to be that marriage was permitted only between a man and a woman. Now the pope and some German prelates appear to be relaxing attitudes and policies about same sex relationships. So, the mores and even the Word of God are subject to change. If one can justify the changes and go along with them, or worse, fail to question them, then they can remain Catholic, but not in the same vein in which they entered the faith in the first place.

The same is true of political parties. Coming from a democratic household, I naturally was a democrat in my early life. In the 50s and 60s that party made sense. It was the party of the working folk and sought what was best for America and Americans. It espoused the values that most people held and generally upheld the principles of the Constitution. It was somewhat evenly balanced between liberalism and conservatism. It was a decent political home. Unrealized at first, that party began to change in the 60s. That decade saw the advent of liberalism in the extreme: free love, the Hippie movement, Woodstock, drug use and the like. Suddenly, everything was okay for this new fringe. Liberalism then took on a life of its own and attached itself to the democrat party. The party slid more and more to the left such that after the advent of 2000 it became the party of progressives. Progressives are identifiable as advocates of globalism, open borders, socialism, decriminalization of many activities, marginalization of law enforcement and erosion of Constitutional guarantees. Liberals, whether democrat or not, have adopted the mantra of postmodernism, i.e. everyone has their own truth regardless of actual truth. Postmodernists see truth as unknowable and therefore flexible and adaptable to whatever they want it to be. This accounts for 1984-isms that construe words to be what they are wanted to mean. Redefinitions are common. Gender can now be self-identified. History can be revised or eradicated. Meaningful pronouns and adjectives can be banned, and words deemed offensive by some cannot be used at great risk to anyone who dares to use them.

The democrat party has undergone great change. Adherents can either wrap themselves in the illusion of what the party once was, ignoring its change, or choose another option. A decision to ignore the change of party character is self-destructive because one is known by the company one keeps. One who adheres to a much-changed party implicitly adopts the shifted paradigm and must be deemed to embrace it. Relevant truths were espoused by Leo Tolstoy: "Disrespect for tradition has not caused a thousandth part of the evil that has been caused by observing traditions, customs and institutions that have become meaningless." "Nothing can interfere with the growth of truth—nothing except the wish to preserve old traditions and prejudices." "The greatest insolence is the establishment by some of a religious law which is to be accepted by all others without discussion or question. Why must people do this?"
Leo Tolstoy: In My Own Words

History teaches us many things. Among the lessons is the fact that entire populations have been led down destructive paths seemingly unaware of what was happening—perhaps clueless or gullible, or maybe unduly influenced by media. Regardless, the people as a whole are judged to have accepted the consequences of political and cultural change. Some examples are:

- Germans in the 1930s and 1940s were seen as complicit in Nazism.
- Catholics in the Middle Ages were seen as complicit in the torture and murder of unbelievers.
- For ages Jews were seen as complicit in the murder of Christ, an event underlying antisemitism.
- Residents of the southern United States in the 1800s were seen as

subjugators of slaves.
- Muslims are seen as complicit in the jihadist activities conducted in the name of Islam.

What needs to be understood and accepted is that change is a fundamental fact of nature and that we must all assess the direction and effects of change and adjust accordingly.

November/December 2018

Tolstoy: A Rebuttal

Leo Tolstoy wrote about love being the supreme law to which humanity must aspire. This theory was that violence has no place in our world and that the way to achieve peace is to change oneself. The change he suggests is that everyone should resist violence; react to violence with love and understanding rather than retaliation or self-defense. In defining his theory, he draws on the teachings of Jesus Christ. He points to Christ's sayings that if someone strikes you, turn the other cheek.

The foundation of his argument appears to be taking Christ's teachings about his kingdom not being of this earth, but by following his lead, his kingdom can be established on earth.

As much as I admire Tolstoy as a great thinker and advocate of compassion and true religion, I am inclined to disagree. Utopia, or heaven on earth, is not possible. The reason is that the principle of polar opposites is the foundation for the entire spectrum of existence, from the simplest cell to the universe itself. And this necessarily includes the Supreme Being. The principle is that all motion is a function of opposing actions. For every step forward that a man takes, one foot goes backward. Democracy exists because of a two-party system of checks and balances. Flora and fauna survive because of changes in the seasons between hot and cold. Species reproduce only because of the existence of paired opposites: male and female.

The god or gods of the bible indicate paired opposites. The god of the Old Testament was a jealous and vindictive entity whereas the god of the New Testament was more benign.

Jesus certainly showed a path toward the ideal of a peaceful and free existence, such as heaven is depicted. However, the reality is that heaven may not be that at all. Take, for example, the revelation that there are legions of both good and bad angels. Polar opposites are needed to propel the universe on a spiritual plane. Take also, for example, that man was created in god's image and likeness, composed of both good and evil. If man truly reflects god, then god must be composed of both good and evil. Does god exist and continue to exist because god is driven as a being comprised of both good and bad elements?

How does this translate into how we humans should conduct ourselves as moral beings? If we are attacked, should be not defend ourselves as Tolstoy proposed?

If our family is about to be slaughtered should we passively submit to the will of a higher authority? If someone steals from me should he not be compelled to suffer some punishment? If someone sets fire to our house should we consent to perish in the flames? Put in Tolstoy's terms, shall a man become so aesthetically sensitized that all is conceded to the willfully harmful intent of others? Tolstoy would say yes, in reliance on Christ's teaching of the law of love having absolutely no exceptions.

Christ, however, was not unaware of the law of the interaction of polar opposites, the yin and the yang, the necessity of bipedalism for forward movement. Even he became angry and drove the money changers out of the temple.

Adhering to the Enemy

Treason against the United States shall consist only in levying War against them, or in adhering to their Enemies, giving them aid and comfort. *U.S. Constitution Article III, Section 3, Clause I.*

How is an enemy defined? An enemy is fundamentally considered to be a foreign entity that attacks or wages war on the United States. An enemy is also a combatant on foreign soil of a nation or country which the United States is defending. But enemy combatants are not the only enemies that seek to undermine or destroy the United States.

Major world powers understand that war is both costly and destructive, even potentially so destructive as to devastate large portions of the world. A country can be wholly destroyed in moments. The deterrent effect of nuclear armaments, however, does not mean that there are no enemies of the United States that would seek to destroy it. There are ways to undermine or even destroy the United States other than declaring or waging war in the traditional sense. For example, Russia is believed to have sought to undermine the 2016 election using social media to influence voters in particular directions with the goal of dividing Americans into competing factions. Perhaps they also used cyber and psychological warfare. Russia was and is an enemy of the United States seeking to undermine this country without use of conventional warfare.

China has infiltrated institutions of higher learning, corporations and even government with the goal of discovering technological advances and corporate and government secrets. American countries that operate in China are forced to share proprietary information. In these ways, China is an enemy of the United States even though there is no overt declaration of war.

Cartels are in effect waging war against the United States, albeit other than in the conventional sense. Cartels are flooding the United States with drugs. They are selling humans into sexual slavery. They are infiltrating the states with criminal gangs. In doing so, the cartels are wreaking havoc in communities throughout the U.S. and as a consequence, draining billions of dollars from the economy. Treasury dollars are required to combat opioids and crime and to provide a multitude of benefits to illegal entrants into the country. Meanwhile, cartels get rich from the proceeds of their criminal enterprise.

If Russia, China, cartels and other entities are enemies of the United States, whether overtly or covertly, do we give them aid and comfort by not taking steps to thwart their efforts? If, for example, we fail to stop cartels at the border from smuggling drugs and sex slaves into the states, are those in charge at least giving them aid? Is not stopping them a form of assistance—facilitating their criminality by failing to take rudimentary precautions? If so, is that not a betrayal of the country and therefore treasonous?

If we, and by "we" I mean Congress, decline to take steps to root out foreign spies in our universities, corporations and government, or to stop illegal activities at our borders, or to thwart foreign power's use of social media against the United States, are we aiding our enemies? If so, it that treasonous? Even if aiding these entities does not amount to treason, does the aiding not amount to collusion, or to aiding and abetting crime? And should not those who engage in collusion, or aiding and abetting, or betraying their oath to uphold the Constitution not face arrest and prosecution?

There could be more concrete examples of treason, or at least collusion. It has been a cartel pattern and practice to achieve their goals with bribery, kidnappings and murder. It has been reported that the former president of Mexico, Enrique Peña Nieto, took a $100-million bribe from Joaquín Guzmán Loera, El Chapo, to forego inconvenient law enforcement. This is according to a witness at El Chalpo's trial. If drug lords target government officials with bribes, how likely is it that U.S. government officials have been offered money or other perquisites so as not to interfere with lucrative cartel business practices? If that has occurred, shouldn't there be investigations and appropriate legal consequences for bribery recipients?

The U.S. is a soft target for organized criminal enterprises. Addicts and sex trade aficionados collectively pay billions of dollars for what the cartels provide. Taxpayers pay billions more treating people affected by rampant crime that could be better controlled by securing the border and revamping immigration law. The United States should be a nation instead of a doormat.

March 12, 2019

Ant Confederacy

The colony leader was wise, having led the colony for many years. He encouraged the workers to maintain the work line and pace and rewarded them with ample time off, good food and with the knowledge that their work was what preserved the colony. For many years they labored without any threats from outside their colony.

Independence was the nature of these colonies. Each colony worked its own territory and fended for itself. One day, however, a distant but related sister colony appeared on the scene. The leader of the newly arrived colony set out new rules for the host colony to follow. There was no consultation, only demands for compliance. The host colony leader refused to comply with the invading colony leader's demands and refused to concede territory or independence from outside interference. Peaceful coexistence was preferred, but war against the invader was understood to be a viable option.

While each colony was independent, they had wisely formed a confederacy, a central form of government designed to afford protection for the colonies against all enemies, whether within the boundaries of the confederacy or outside of it. The colonies elected those from within its ranks who would staff the confederacy and speak for them in the making of rules and other matters of governance. The confederacy proceeded to issue rules intended for the common good, rules that would recognize the longstanding work processes and ethics of colony workers and protect them from aggression from other colonies or other enemies.

Over time, some colonies became more powerful that others in terms of the rules that would be made. Eventually, a powerful elected leader broke from tradition and decided that the confederacy did not need to be protected from enemies from outside the confederacy. Members of colonies from outside the confederacy were fleeing from the confines of colonies that were less than beneficent, from colonies that had been corrupted by greedy and self-serving leaders. Some of the fleeing colonists themselves had been corrupted and had turned to trafficking drugs and even less fortunate colonists to sustain lives that did not require the work of traditional colonists. They saw the confederacy as the ideal place to ply their evil trade yet enjoy the protection of the confederacy.

The corrupt confederacy leader did not believe that the foreign colonists should be denied entry into the confederacy because of their destitute status, but declining to concede that many of them were evil and would destroy the fabric of the confederacy that was working well, with all of the colonies in sync with each other. This leader refused to permit a rule that the main elected leader thought would stem the invading foreign colonists. That leader wanted to build a wall to keep the confederacy safe and preserve the way of life that had worked so well for centuries. The wall was not built, the invaders overwhelmed the Confederacy, and the Confederacy devolved such that there was no distinction between the Confederacy and the confederacies that the invaders had fled.

January 24, 2019

Ejection of God from the Public Square

Imagine if you were God and your creatures forbade any homage to or mention of you. If mankind were arrogant enough to think that man created God rather than the other way around, that man is smarter than God, what do you think the reaction would be?

History reveals that God has softened somewhat in his approach to meting out punishment. Certainly, a substantial amount of time has been allowed for man to repent. What, we may ask, does God have in store for the America that has banned him from almost every venue? Perhaps God has fashioned a punishment that fits the crime—draconian, but not irreversible. Perhaps he is facilitating the takeover of America by Islam. If so, God is thinking not of death and destruction, but of imposition of a set of values exactly the opposite of those held dear in the America of today. Islam abhors female flesh. Gone will be Hollywood's pursuit of revenue from display of naked and near naked women. Would-be stars and starlets would be wearing burkas rather than bikinis. Gone also would be TV shows featuring women, porn and soft porn, and all potential influences on viewers that are not consistent with Islam.

Christianity would be replaced with Islam. Churches have not stood up to decry the fouling of American culture. Therefore, they would be deprived of icons of the Christian religion, such as the Ten Commandments, the crucifix, ornate churches—everything that has been dear to churches over the past few hundred years. Christian churches will become mosques.

10/26/13

Times of Our Life

When we are toddlers everyone loves us. They invariably think we are cute and cuddly. We are cared for, nourished and taught as we grew. When we became teens, we were objects of worry about the mistakes we would make and the dangers we would face. When we were young adults, we were encouraged to learn a trade or profession and to become responsible. In midlife we were busy building families and careers. Those who cared about us were encouraging and supportive but left us alone to chart our own paths. Most people who came into our lives sought our advice, counsel or craftsmanship. They were in our lives only for the short time it took to service their needs. Some stayed in our lives longer, a few as friends and even fewer as family. Life has been filled with business and busyness and this paradigm holds true up to retirement. We meet and accept challenges that we devote all resources to overcome.

It is commonly opined that we work so that we can retire and enjoy the fruits of our labor. Retirement, however, can be the greatest challenge of all. While we spend our lives working, our value lies in our productivity, our being needed by other people or organizations, our worth measured in terms of how we interact with our customers, clients or employers. When we retire, our reliance on these pillars stops. The loss of these pillars requires psychological adaptation. We realize that our worth, as previously measured on our work life, is largely gone. Certainly, there may be calls upon us for our historical or specialized knowledge, but even this remnant of worth erodes over a relatively short period of time. The challenge then becomes how to adapt and establish a new paradigm of worth, or worthiness.

The challenge is not an easy one. For many, what we did in the world of work defines who we are or who we became. Retirement can seem like an exercise in throwing that identity away. Our knowledge, talents, expertise and experience have become irrelevant. What does one have to do to cope with this change? As a first step, one must acknowledge that retirement is a much different world in which past associations lapse for lack of commonality, one's experience and expertise is no longer needed, that we are no longer needed in our prior world. Then we slowly and grudgingly realize that our minds and our bodies no longer enjoy prior unfettered freedoms as our minds and bodies succumb to the advancement of age. We must accept these changes as part of life. Time marches on while our minds and bodies lag. So, where do we find a new sense of worth?

Over the course of a life we have acquired wisdom. Wisdom can and should be shared. But the problem is that those closest to us are often unwilling to listen to our counsel. Children, grandchildren and even spouses know better. Our wisdom is "outdated." Wisdom is misperceived because it resides in us old fogies. Wisdom isn't hip or *avant garde*. We continue to try, however, because our mission is to make life better for those who follow us.

Our wisdom can be shared with others. Anyone willing to listen can benefit from our wisdom and counsel. By sharing our wisdom, gained through life experiences, we can keep others from making the same mistakes that we made.

One of the most difficult aspect of growing older is our lack of relevance. When we become unable to care for ourselves, we become not just irrelevant but a burden. We become the proverbial dead man walking. We become dependent on others to do what we can no longer do. At best, we are cared for in our home by family or visiting nurses and caregivers. At worst, we are confined to an assisted living facility or a skilled nursing facility where we await death without dignity. To deal with this part of life, one can adopt an attitude of valiance, that is, treating it as an object or event to be overcome. Face it with a combination of graceful acceptance, an attitude of "damn the torpedoes, full speed ahead," a battle to be fought and won, use of humor, and a forward-looking vision of the hereafter. We recognize that we are no longer the cute little baby but an older version of the same person. We simply morph like a butterfly and wing our way to eternity.

July 2019

Disrespectful Celebrity Activity

I was a lifelong sports fan, especially of football, baseball and boxing. During football season I spent my Sundays watching the pro football matchups. Then during an ESPN halftime show, maybe a decade ago, Bob Costas presumed to lecture viewers on the evils of firearms. At that point I vowed to turn off the TV whenever Mr. Costas was to appear. Then, as sports coverage turned more and more to political diatribe, I refused to watch any halftime shows. Then, when Colin Kaepernick dissed the American Flag and National Anthem by kneeling, I vowed to cut my addiction to pro sports cold turkey. So, with great reluctance, I stopped watching sports and returned to Sundays devoted to things other than watching sports.

I continue to be offended by the antics of sports figures, no matter how athletically proficient. Given the narcissistic antics of the women's soccer champions, I'm so repulsed that I will not be watching women's soccer matches. Sports are for entertainment, not political or other proselytization.

Because Kaepernick objected to Nike's honoring Betsy Ross with images of her flag on its sneakers, and because Nike caved to his objection, I have vowed never to purchase Nike products. I don't believe in mass boycotts of businesses because of their political or religious leanings. However, I reserve the right to express my individual opposition to businesses I consider unworthy of my patronage. I also will not patronize businesses that adopt policies that interfere with my constitutional rights. In this vein are retail stores that refuse to continue selling firearms or that support draconian government laws and regulations. I also will not patronize businesses that cave to organized boycotts that are tantamount to blackmail.

The best way to deal with the PC celebs and PC dictators is to simply ignore them. Conduct business and live life as if they did not exist.

7/13/19

The Fart Heard 'Round the World

There was an item in the news about a Florida woman who farted loudly in a checkout line of some store. The male customer to her rear complained. Apparently offended by the complaint, the woman made a further stink by pulling a knife with which she proceeded to assault the complainer. The incident quickly gained worldwide attention.

This is a matter of attitude. On my office wall is a plaque to remind me of its importance. It says:

> "ATTITUDE: The little difference in people is attitude. The big difference in people is whether it is positive or negative."

What do people's attitude say about them? What does a narcissistic attitude broadcast to the world convey about Americans' attitude?

This episode speaks volumes about how American culture has sunk. It says to the world that we are so narcissistic that we can assault or offend anyone and then get perturbed at anyone who complains. In other words, I can assault or offend you, but you better not complain because I have the right to do anything I want. Furthermore, if you complain and stand in the way, you are going to pay dearly for that. It's a culture of "it's all about me." I can break the rules; I can assault your senses; I can trample on your rights and sensibilities; but don't you dare call me out. What a great symbol of America! This was much more that a fart. It was a smear on America. Once again, we are the *Ugly American*. The view of this incident conveyed to the world is that America stinks.

By way of disclaimer, I have not seen a picture of the incident participants, so I do not know the race, national origin, religion or other characteristics of the flatulent customer. The reporting was that the farter was a woman, but who knows how she identifies sexually or if he/she is a transgender. By writing this piece I cannot, therefore, be labelled as a racist, sexist, misogynist, or any other "ist."

8/22/19

The Bastardization of Language

Language evolves over time as does everything else. Evolution is part of the grand scheme of nature. But use of language does not need to devolve into meaninglessness. Language will evolve on its own and does not need remodeling for political correctness. Concepts of humor, metaphors, parody, irony, similes, alliteration, allegory and hyperbole, especially hyperbole and humor, are not understood or not deemed acceptable means of communication in current American society.

In the current environment, words spoken sometimes decades ago cause people the loss of their livelihood, awards and influence. That is not right, as context is necessary to understanding both current and past language usage.

Language is being attacked in America. Freedom of speech is being severely eroded such that we cannot use certain words once they offend someone for just about any reason. Someone objects to a word and then it must be banned. As an example, there once was a drive-thru hamburger restaurant doing business as Murder Burger. It was pretty good and stood for years until someone who lost a family member to murder complained that the drive-thru's moniker revived unpleasant memories and demanded that the name be changed. The company caved and changed its name to REDRUM, "murder" spelled in reverse. Many saw the cave-in as spinelessness and patronage declined.

Consider the word "owner" now, as in the owner of a sports team. Some demand that this word not be used because it harkens back to those who owned slaves, and that since many professional team athletes are black, the "owner of blacks are racist." That, despite that the athletes are multi-millionaires and have nothing in common with slaves. We're talking here of sensibilities over sense.

Words matter. To the extent that specified words cannot be used, the right of free speech is degraded. Condemnation of any word is the beginning of a rush to condemn any word or phrase that could cause discomfort. Ultimately language could be so restricted that discourse becomes impossible. Gone are the days when analogies, figures of speech, acronyms, nicknames, and so forth are understood as intended and not as an insult or as something wholly unintended. People were once able to distinguish between tongue-in-cheek humor and malevolent speech, but now everything is taken as malevolent and is either intentionally misunderstood or the product of stupidity. Context is ignored and malevolent intent is assumed. Otherwise good intentions are deliberately misconstrued. Evil is presumed as underlying every expression. A misinterpreted statement or joke can destroy a person's career and end their livelihood. Today, someone who is not familiar with the proliferation of gender pronouns can use a "wrong" one, draw a complaint and lose his or her job—all because of faux offense over a probably confused mindset or the lack of now required re-learning.

What is worse is that what is deemed acceptable depends on who utters an offensive word. Most Americans recognize that use of the "f" word is inappropriate and substitute "freakin'" to avoid insensitivity. But when a soccer star publicly says she won't go the "f…ng" White House, or a congresswoman yells, "Impeach the "m…fer," that is somehow given a pass. Regardless, it demeans the team or the constituency and demeans America as well. Those given a public platform must be held to a higher standard of behavior.

It is a given in America that our Constitution protects speech, no matter how offensive. Challenges to uses of words, redefinition of words and banning usage of words is a subtle erosion of the First Amendment protections and an incremental eroding of the Constitution. Word policing is a slippery slope that undermines the fabric of our society.

Examples of the bastardization of language abound:
Progressive legislatures are enacting unconstitutional language demands and academia is engineering language overhauls. Reproduced here is an article by the *Associated Press* dated 7/17/19:

"No 'manpower': Berkeley bans gender-specific words in code
"BERKELEY, Calif. — Berkeley, California, has adopted an ordinance to replace some terms with gender-neutral words in the city code.

> "The *San Francisco Chronicle* reports Wednesday that 'she' and 'he' will be replaced by 'they.' The words 'manpower' and 'manhole' will become 'workforce' and 'maintenance hole.'
>
> "The City Council on Tuesday unanimously passed the measure to replace more than two dozen commonly used terms. There will be no more 'craftsmen' in city code, only 'craftspeople' or 'artisans.'"

The upshot of this ordinance is to require mental reprogramming. Doesn't this embody the horror predicted in Orwell's *1984*? Forced "evolution" of language is no evolution at all.

On July 18, 2019, Bill O'Reilly commented about University of Colorado at Boulder. He noted the words that you don't use on campus:

> "You can't say the word 'male.' 'Female,' 'Ladies and gentlemen' or 'Mr., Mrs., or Miss.' Why? Quote: 'Male and female refers to biological sex and not gender. In terms of communication methods, we very rarely need to identify or know a person's biological sex and we more often refer to gender.' So, you don't need to know if you're talking about a person whether they're male or female? A man or a woman? A lady or a gentleman? You don't need to know? In other words, CSU they don't want you to use 'straight.' The word implies that anyone LGBT is crooked. OK. Other words. Oh God. Cakewalk. I don't know why. 'Eeny meeny miney mo' is out. 'Freshman' is out because it has MAN in it. Hip-hip hooray. 'Hold down the fort' is out because it gives it a militaristic meaning. 'Policeman' is out because it contains the word 'man.' Handicapped parking also should not be used. It minimizes personhood and offends disabled people. Now this is fascism of course. Which it is. CSU is going to tell you, how you... have to talk. What words you can and cannot say."

O'Reilly has nailed it.

Colorado State University has developed an Inclusive Language Guide. That guide lists more than 100 words or phrases that they urge to be dumped into the dust bin of history. Examples include:

> Any word that has "man" in it needs to be reconfigured, e.g. "freshman" is now "first year."

"epileptic," which is a medical term, is now to be recast as "person with seizure disorder."

"I'm starving" must be reduced to "I'm hungry."

"Paraplegic," which is a medical term, is to be replaced with "person with a spinal cord injury."

The university has ascribed allegedly historical meanings to words and phrases that few, if any, people ever thought of. Use of language does not need to devolve into meaninglessness.

Consider the insanity of San Francisco transmogrification of common language. Now a "convicted felon or an offender released from jail" must now be called a "formerly incarcerated person" or a "justice-involved person" or simply a "returning resident." Repeat offenders will be called "addicts." Actual drug addicts must be called "a person with a history of substance use." This is nothing more than a game of hide-and-seek, but not the kind of childhood game that was actually fun. They hide the meaning in new words or phrases, and we have to find the meaning. A "justice-involved person" can include judges, attorneys, bailiffs, other court personnel and police. The new designation can reduce justice workers to felons or raise felons to the status of court personnel. If we can't talk using commonly understood words and terms, actual meaning and facts are of no consequence. This form of homogenization just doesn't work. Discourse is unavoidably stymied when one needs to carefully choose words that might offend someone or some group.

There are those who look behind every tree and under every rock to find some form of racism. Even the *Lion King* is not exempt. One writer who stretched to find racism theorized that the movie reflects a society that is unequal and therefore racist. The theory is that the lions symbolize the ruling class; the herbivores symbolize society's decent, law-abiding citizens (underlings); and the hyenas represent the minority of black, brown, disabled and others that are marginalized or even excluded from society. Why not just enjoy the show instead of demonizing it with critiques that most would not notice or care about?

The forced "evolution" of the English language will have results, some of which are dangerous. Some will rebel and vow never to accede to the language and thought police. Some will simply ignore the demands that they adapt to the new language codes. These people will likely succumb to the traps and wrath of the language/thought police. Thoughtful people with a job, a career, a business, or who are involved in politics will consider their use of words and language carefully out of fear that they could lose their livelihood, position and reputation. They realize that the language/thought police will excommunicate them from their job or career, ruin their business and reputation, and perhaps even have them jailed. The inherent danger is that the right of free speech is not just chilled, but frozen. They will not speak out of fear and so the possibilities of meaningful dialogue are stifled.

Another danger is that people will withdraw into their TV, cell phones, iPods, iPads and computers in order to avoid human interactions and speech that might harm them. In sum, forced language changes, word and phrase prohibitions, and other pronouncements of the righteous and politically correct will not advance American culture, but would destroy it. These scenarios are all lose-lose propositions. We must remain vigilant to protect our Constitutional freedoms and this means attending to the proper use of words and phrases and ignoring attacks on longstanding and common understandings of English words and phrases. Use of language should be a joy rather than a burden.

Word policing is a slippery slope that undermines the fabric of our society. Pardon those of us who will continue to use common words, continue to support the First Amendment, and to symbolically flip off, I mean castigate, the thought and word police.

8/24/19

The Hare and the Hounds

A rabbit has staked out a spot on our neighbor's property. It sits there day after day, maintaining control of that piece of ground. Our dogs, when let outside, bark wildly at the rabbit. The barking has no effect on the rabbit. The rabbit stands its ground and the dogs never realize that no matter how long or how loud they bark, the rabbit remains unfazed.

This real-life situation is a metaphor for President Trump and the rabble that attacks his every word or action. The President is the rabbit who stands his ground. No matter how long and how vicious his detractors yap and howl, it doesn't affect him. He stands his ground and does what he believes is the right thing to do.

The President is the king of the hill. ("King of the hill" is an allusion to a game played by children of an earlier generation and is used here as a metaphor. Use of "president" and "king" in the same sentence is not meant to infer that the President is acting like a king.) It's trite but true, that the very fact that there is a king of the hill means that there are many who want to tear the king off the hill and replace him. All fail to realize that once one is on top of the hill, the masses will seek to tear him down from the hill. To remain on the hill, and to remain unfazed by the attacking hordes, is astonishing in that it defies both history and the nature of man.

8/25/19

PART IV
SONG, PARODIES, and HUMOR

America (My Country, 'Tis of Thee)

Text: Samuel F. Smith, 1808-1895
Music: Thesaurus Musicus
Tune: AMERICA, Meter: 664.6664

1. My country, 'tis of thee,
   sweet land of liberty, of thee I sing;
   land where my fathers died,
   land of the pilgrims' pride,
   from every mountainside let freedom ring!

2. My native country, thee,
   land of the noble free, thy name I love;
   I love thy rocks and rills,
   thy woods and templed hills;
   my heart with rapture thrills, like that above.

3. Let music swell the breeze,
   and ring from all the trees sweet freedom's song;
   let mortal tongues awake;
   let all that breathe partake;
   let rocks their silence break, the sound prolong.

4. Our fathers' God, to thee,
   author of liberty, to thee we sing;
   long may our land be bright
   with freedom's holy light;
   protect us by thy might, great God, our King.

Parody Follows
America (My Country 'Tis of Me)[2]
(as sung by Barack Hussein Obama II)

This country, 'tis of me
This land that once was free
Of me I sing.
Land where your fathers died
Is now our Muslims' pride
Since liberty and freedom died
Let Sharia guide.

Not my native country, thee,
Land that once was free, thy name I hate;
I hate thy rocks and rills,
Thy woods and templed hills;
My heart with rapture thrills, as your freedom dies.

Let my economy turn the tide,
Let all your tongues be still,
With no more cars to ride;
May all your wants be laid aside
Let us your liberty deride, a wondrous sound.

Let us your Constitution smite
Let Sharia law prevail,
Negative covenants are not right
Only Sharia law is right
You must submit without a fight.

Your fathers' god is not my god
We'll worship Allah, praise his name
Long may this land be bright
And Sharia law be swift and right.
Protect me by thy might great god, Allah.

---

[2] With apologies to Samuel F. Smith, 1808-1895, original author of *America, My Country, 'Tis of Thee*.

Your fathers' god is god no more
Allah's your god forevermore;
Mohammed died for all afar
Not Jesus Christ, your superstar!
With Sharia's holy light
Protect us, oh great God, Allah.

August 22, 2010

Taliban Parody

(sung to Harry Belafonte's "Day-O")

Hey there, Taliban, Taliban abusers
Daylight come and abuse some more.

One sister, two sister, three sister four
One get raped and they call her a whore
One that's a "whore" she live no more.

Hey there, Taliban, Taliban abusers
Woman not a virgin, she not live anymore.

February 14, 1999

Unions: The Sound of Fright

(sung to the tune of "My Favorite Things" from *The Sound of Music*)

Punches on noses and pokes in the eyes
Breaking of bones and tearing of eyes
Brass knuckle sandwiches; sharp finger rings
These are the union thugs' favorite things

Patches of purple on innocent faces
Fractures, contusions on most other places
Wild fists that fly with lightning stings
These are the union goons' favorite things

Girls in stained dresses from union thug slashes
Blood clots sticking on nose and eyelashes
People with faces that sport major stings
These are the union thugs' favorite things.

When the goons bite
When they're causing fright
When they're causing pain
They gladly remember their favorite things
Then do it all over again.

December 2012

Christmas in Smoke

'Twas the night before Christmas, but because of the smog
Not a creature was breathing, not even a frog.
Wife in her nightgown and I in my shorts
Had just settled down, having had a few snorts.

A fire was roaring up the chimney quite fast.
We had just curled up and were napping at last.
A spark flew out, caught the curtain on fire.
The flames started up, then leaped higher and higher.

When what to my wondering eyes should appear
But a red fire engine with oxygen gear.
The firemen rushed to our sides with air
In hopes that our lives they could save with their care.

The masks to our faces were strapped with a string.
The flow of the oxygen thrilled my ears with a ring.
As the oxygen started, I breathed with a sigh
But how I wished I could see some blue sky.

The medic looked down and stated with glee
That Christmas would be here in a minute or three.
Reached into his pocket and drew out a smoke.
He lighted it up and I thought I would choke.

He gave it to me with the thought it would help.
I tried to say "no," but my lips felt like kelp.
I gasped for some air and fought for a breath
But all I could get was a taste of my death.

A fireman leaned over and breathed in my ear:
"Merry Christmas to you, may you have a good year."
Then I heard him exclaim as he walked from the room:
"The fact he can't smoke is what's sealed his doom."

I knew we were doomed without some fresh air.
I tried to be brave but felt only despair.
Then up in the sky there came such a clatter
My startled brain wakened to see what was the matter.

The lightning flashed and the rain started falling
And all of a sudden I heard my wife calling.
"Honey, wake up, you've had some bad dreaming—
A minute ago you were yelling and screaming."

Cat and Mouse

Cat and mouse
Cat and mouse
Chasing all around the house.

Mouse in hole
Cat outside
Goddamn cat just sat and cried.

Mouse in hole
Cat outside
Mouse just laughed and held his side.

1964

Who's the Dummy?

Ventriloquist (V) to Dummy Al (A)

V   Good evening, sir. I'll be your ventriloquist this evening.
A   Glad to meet ya.
V   My name is Ben.
A   My name is Al, Al Cada.
V   You gotta be kidding. How can your name be Al Qaida?
A   It is. I'm Al Cada. Have been since birth.
V   But Al Qaida is a terrorist organization. Are you a terrorist?
A   No, I'm not an organization and I'm not a terrorist. But I am Al Cada.
V   OK. Knock it off. You can't be Al Qaida. Al Qaida kills people and explodes bombs. Do you bomb?
A   I only bomb when I'm on stage and the joke doesn't work.
V   OK, wise guy. Do you believe in the Prophet? Do you follow the Prophet?
A   Aren't we doing this show for profit? I thought that's what this was all about. Don't you work for profit?
B   Are you a believer in Allah?
V   I do like my meals served a la carte once in a while.

January 17, 2015

PART V
DEDICATION

In closing, I dedicate this work in honor of my grandmother, Zoe Caroline (Patrick) Fitzgerald. She was a very wise woman and a great inspiration. To honor her memory, I am including poems that she wrote.

Advice for a Happy Life

Be always as merry
as ever you can,
For no one delights
in a sorrowful man.

Keep your temper;
no one else wants it.

Trust Him.
Trust Him when dark doubts assail thee;
Trust Him when thy strength is small,
Trust Him when to simply trust Him
Seems the hardest thing of all.

Smile.
Sometimes when you're feeling blue,
Stop! Then think awhile,
How many times you wonder why
You think you cannot smile.

It's not so hard to smile at a thing;
Just try it out sometime;
It may be hard at first, you see,
But then you will incline.

It is better not to smile at all,
If smiling takes an act of will;
Smiles are a product of the heart,
And should not be a mask for ill.

Learn to smile.

Zoe Caroline (Patrick) Fitzgerald (date unknown but before 1963)

Glory

All glory to Thee
Holy Babe,
In the manger lined with hay!
'Twas the star-bright light that led me
On a long and trying way…
To find,
To know,
To worship Thee
And be filled with peace and joy
To see my King and Savior
In this
Little Baby Boy.

Zoe Caroline (Patrick) Fitzgerald (1956)